MANAGING
ORGANIZATIONAL
CONFLICT

MANAGING ORGANIZATIONAL CONFLICT

A Nontraditional Approach

STEPHEN P. ROBBINS

Associate Professor and Chairman
Department of Management
Sir George Williams University
Montreal, Canada

PRENTICE-HALL, INC., Englewood Cliffs, New Jersey

59947

Library of Congress Cataloging in Publication Data

ROBBINS, STEPHEN P   1943-
   Managing organizational conflict.

   Bibliography: p.
   1. Management.   2. Industrial sociology.
3. Social conflict.   I. Title.
HD38.R57   658.4   73-22343
ISBN   0-13-550491-0
ISBN   0-13-550483-X (pbk.)

Printed in the United States of America

10   9   8   7   6   5   4   3   2

PRENTICE-HALL INTERNATIONAL, INC., *London*
PRENTICE-HALL OF AUSTRALIA, PTY. LTD., *Sydney*
PRENTICE-HALL OF CANADA, LTD., *Toronto*
PRENTICE-HALL OF INDIA PRIVATE LIMITED, *New Delhi*
PRENTICE-HALL OF JAPAN, INC., *Tokyo*

TO ALIX, DANA, AND JENNIFER

Contents

2

An Interactionist Approach

Philosophies of Conflict
Value of Conflict
Survival Requires Change
Paradox of Conflict
Summary

3

A Point of Departure

Definition
Functional Versus Dysfunctional
Competition
Cooperation
Summary

II

SOURCES OF CONFLICT

4

Communications

Communication Model
Sources of Communication Distortion
Semantic Difficulties
Ambiguity Versus Perfect Knowledge
Channels
Summary

5

Structure

Size
Bureaucratic Qualities
Heterogeneity of Staff
Style of Supervision

9

Stimulation Techniques   78

IV

MANAGING CONFLICT

10

Model Development   93

11

Recapitulation   112

APPENDIX

Preface

Social conflict has become an increasingly important part of studies in organization and administrative theory. No current investigation of how organizations operate is complete without an understanding of the significance of conflict and the techniques for its management.

I have searched extensively to locate a comprehensive source on social conflict that could supplement my courses in Administrative Theory and Organizational Behavior. What I found was either incomplete or intended for psychology or sociology curriculums, not for the student of administration. Clearly, something is needed to fill the void that exists between the wealth of material on administration and the theoretical approaches to conflict developed by social scientists.

This book is designed to meet that need. The management of conflict is relevant to both theorist and practitioner. Although I work within a theoretical framework, numerous illustrations have been included to satisfy the need for relevance and application. Further, the ideas expressed in this book are intended for all students of administration and management, regardless of specialization. The material is appropriate to those who manage in a variety of organizations: business, educational, governmental, military, medical, or ecclesiastical. It can be utilized as an effective supplement to any course that is primarily involved with the management of human resources:

Human Relations, Organizational Behavior or Theory, Innovation and Change, Administrative Theory, or as a stimulating adjunct to a Fundamentals of Management course.

This book makes some strong attacks on contemporary assumptions underlying conflict and its management. Rather than being a summary of other treatises, it represents a major departure in conflict thought and has challenged the traditional view of conflict's role in organizations. More specifically, I have questioned those who have historically defined conflict management as synonymous with conflict resolution. My definition is expanded to include a vital new dimension—stimulation.

I hasten to add that this book is only a beginning to a new perspective of conflict management. Hopefully, my thoughts will encourage others to actively manage conflict through planning and evaluating its impact and, further, to develop new and better techniques for its stimulation and resolution.

Those to whom I am indebted for contributions to this book are too numerous to mention in this preface. However, I wish to single out Professor Kenneth H. Blanchard, University of Massachusetts, Professor Louis R. Desfosses, University of Rhode Island, Professor Peter A. Raynolds, University of Southern California, and Professor E. C. Wegner, University of Saskatchewan, Regina Campus, for their helpful comments and suggestions.

I would especially like to thank Professors Michael J. Jucius and Edwin B. Flippo of the University of Arizona for "turning me on" to the excitement of management as a field of study; to Professor John R. Anstey of the University of Nebraska at Omaha for his stimulating thoughts and suggestions as the manuscript developed; to Kathy Schmid for her rapid and accurate typing, and most of all to my wife, Alix, for her assistance and support throughout the entire project.

Stephen P. Robbins

MANAGING
ORGANIZATIONAL
CONFLICT

I

INTRODUCTION

The first three chapters of this book form the base upon which the remainder is developed. Our purpose in Part I is to clarify managing, social conflict, and the role managing social conflict plays in organizations.

The first chapter describes the functions of a manager, which are planning, organizing, leading, and evaluating the performance of others to accomplish objectives.

Chapter 2 reviews three philosophies that describe the nature of conflict in organizations and reinforces the importance of conflict to organizational life.

Chapter 3 brings conflict into perspective by reviewing the term's various definitions and connotations. Specific attention is directed to comparing conflict with the terms competition and cooperation; the former frequently used as a synonym and the latter as an antonym for conflict.

1

The Role of

an Administrator

Those who have the responsibility for deciding the direction an organization will take and who hold the authority to move it toward its goals are the single most important factor in determining an organization's success or failure. Whether in business, education, government, medicine, or religion, the quality of an organization's administrators will determine its success. Successful administrators will anticipate change, vigorously exploit opportunities, correct poor performance, and lead the organization toward its objectives. In contrast to other groups within the organization, administrators have the greatest opportunities to turn straw to gold or to admirably perform the reverse process.

Since administration is the key to an organization's success, its meaning and usage should be clarified. Many writers specifically differentiate administration from management. Although differences can be noted, to avoid semantic confusion we will use the words interchangeably. Most often we will use "administration," because as a discipline it has generally wider appeal than management, and for those who recognize the breadth of the field, it is more readily acceptable. Administration is the universal process of getting things done with and through other people and need not be modified according to the nature of the organization (i.e., business, educational, or public administration). Further, there is no need to assume a profit motive as is often done when referring to management.

Three distinct criteria define the role of an administrator in an organization. The first is the creation of and adherence to a set of goals. Activity must be directed toward some end. The goals that are established need not be explicit, but in those instances where they are non-existent, there is no need for administration.

Second, there must be limited resources. Economic resources by definition are scarce; therefore, the administrator is responsible for their allocation. This efficiency factor requires the administrator not only to be effective—that is, to achieve the goal or goals that are established —but additionally necessitates that he relate output to input. He seeks a given output with less input than now being utilized; or for a given input, he will strive for a greater output. Therefore, the administrator is concerned with attaining goals, which will make him effective, and with the least allocation of scarce resources, which will make him efficient.

The need for two or more people is the third and last prerequisite for administration. It is with and through people that administrators perform their work. The legendary Robinson Crusoe could not have become an administrator until Friday arrived.

In summary, administrators work through people and allocate scarce resources to achieve goals. Should any one of these criteria be missing, there is no need for administration. From a different perspective, we can define administration in functional terms: It is planning, organizing, leading, and evaluating the performance of others toward specific ends. Our goals are determined in the planning function. Allocation of scarce resources is the principal factor in both planning and organizing. Leading is achieving the goals through people. And finally, the evaluation function reviews performance against the goals earlier established and then initiates corrective action, if it is necessary.

The remainder of this chapter briefly surveys the administrator's role in functional terms. For those who have previously studied administration or management, these next few pages can be skimmed quickly. For others, they are provided as a foundation upon which the remaining ten chapters are built.[1]

[1] For a comprehensive investigation of an administrator's role, see:

Edwin Flippo, *Management: A Behavioral Approach* (2nd ed.) (Boston: Allyn & Bacon, 1970).

Michael Jucius, Bernard A. Deitzer, and William E. Schlender, *Elements of Managerial Action* (3rd ed.) (Homewood, Ill.: Richard D. Irwin, Inc., 1973).

Harold Koontz and Cyril O'Donnell, *Principles of Management: An Analysis of Managerial Functions* (5th ed.) (New York: McGraw-Hill Book Co., 1972).

George R. Terry, *Principles of Management* (6th ed.) (Homewood, Ill.: Richard D. Irwin, Inc., 1972).

PLANNING

Planning is determining in advance the objectives and the means by which objectives may be accomplished. It is the deciding in advance what to do, how to do it, and who is to do it. Because it bridges the gap from the present status to future goals, it is the most basic of the four functions. Because it requires determination in advance of action, decision making occurs throughout the function, but decision making alone is not planning.

Planning begins with the establishment of clear objectives. All organizations will have more than a single objective, which requires the determination of a consistent multiple set of major objectives. These should cover economic, service, and social dimensions of the organization. These objectives will set the parameters for administrators to determine if the ongoing activities of members are making positive contributions to the organization.

The multifarious objectives are illustrated by a moderate-sized Midwestern insurance company. Discussions with their management indicated that in addition to an adequate profit, the firm was concerned with improving their market position, generating new and innovative policies, developing a strong and consistent upward trend in revenues, and upgrading the company image with the public and within the insurance industry. Additionally, numerous other subobjectives evolved from these major ones.

Once the reason for the organization's existence is made clear through the statement of major objectives, administrators will establish subobjectives and formulate forecasts. The two interact with each other. The setting of subobjectives influences forecasts and forecasts in turn have an impact on subobjectives.

Forecasting is the process of gathering data and developing assumptions about the future. Information must be gathered and assumptions made regarding external and internal variables. External variables include such considerations as government fiscal and monetary policies; growth in the Gross National Product; and changes in price levels, population trends, and technology. Internal variables consider demand for the organization's product or service, and the factor markets of land, labor, and capital.

Besides decision making, objective setting, and forecasting, planning additionally requires supporting plans. These plans will include the establishment of policies, procedures, methods, standards, and rules.

An administrator's knowledge of his organization's objectives is not sufficient to guide him in the decisions he makes. Further guidelines are necessary so that he can determine the parameters in which he may decide. Policies exist to meet these needs. They do not specify the decisions to be made but set discretionary limits for the decision maker. By developing statements that include ambiguous terms (i.e., best, satisfied, competitive), interpretation is left to the administrator.

The statement from the personnel manual at a major midwestern hospital that it will "pay competitive wages" illustrates a policy. This personnel policy does not tell the Wage and Salary Administrator what he should pay, but gives direction to the decision he will make. The term "competitive" is vague, yet sets discretionary limits. If other local hospitals are paying between $2.60 and $3.20 an hour for an inexperienced orderly, hourly rates of $2.10 or $4.60 would clearly not be within the guidelines set by hospital personnel policy.

The freedom of interpretation that exists in policies does not exist with procedures, methods, standards, and rules. These supporting plans are more specific in stating expected behavior. Procedures define a series of steps for accomplishing a given project. A method is one of the steps of a procedure. Standards state criteria to which things can be compared, in either quantitative or qualitative terms. Finally, rules are the most definite type of plan because they state definite action and leave no room for decision making.

These four types of supporting plans are used in all complex organizations. Each contributes to objectives by narrowly defining behavior. They make the completion of tasks consistent, accurate, and hopefully faster than an undefined operation. They make the training of new employees simpler. And, very importantly, they free the administrator from making a multitude of repetitive decisions.

ORGANIZING

Organizing is the establishment of relationships between the activities to be performed, the personnel to perform them, and the physical factors that are needed. To coordinate the resources one is given, the administrator designs a formal structure of task and authority relationships that will foster the effective and efficient attainment of goals. The major concern in organizing is the dividing up of the jobs to be done, determining the grouping of work, forming authority grades, and equalizing authority and responsibility.

Since the writings of Adam Smith, 200 years ago, we have recognized the potential to increase productivity dramatically through the division of work. By having individuals specialize in very few tasks, get-ready and put-away time is reduced, greater skills are developed, and higher work speeds attained. The automobile assembly line illustrates the value of specialization in manufacturing, as does the surgeon, gynecologist, or nose and throat specialist in the provision of medical services. Throughout history the maturation of organizations has been dependent upon developing individuals with increasingly higher degrees of skills who perform more and more specialized activities. Recently, however, considerable concern has been expressed that the pendulum may have swung too far creating some highly dehumanizing work environments. Whereas highly specialized jobs are efficient, the benefits of specialization are more than offset by the boredom and fatigue that workers are forced to endure. An increasing amount of evidence from studies being conducted supports job enlargement, rather than contraction, as a means to improve productivity.

As organizational members developed greater specialization, it became necessary to determine the number of individuals who would report to an immediate superior. The number of individuals the manager can successfully coordinate ranges from some number greater than one to something obviously less than infinity. The span of management defines the number of subordinates a manager can effectively direct. Depending on the activities performed, the skills of the subordinates, their educational level, experience, and other variables, some managers can effectively direct forty, whereas other managers are fully employed supervising three. The decision regarding this span will directly influence the number of levels in the organizational hierarchy and hence its complexity.

Recognition that no one man can manage an unlimited number of subordinates makes it necessary to break work activities into governable segments. The objectives, outlined in the planning function, determine the tasks that must be performed. These tasks are combined into activities and the activities joined together to create departments. Defining methods of departmentation are key determinants in organization design and the potential interaction between members. Traditional criteria for departmentation include the customer serviced, geographic location, product processes used, and functions performed.

Finally, we want to mention the relationship between authority and responsibility. A graduation of authority is found in all organizations. The scalar principle of organization delineates the flow of authority through the chain of command and results in the vertical growth of the structure. Through delegation of this authority, top management empowers middle and lower level executives with means to achieve their objectives. Designing our organizations so there exists an equality between authority and responsibility insures that the rights to enact compliance are balanced with the expectations of performance.

LEADING

In the leading function we guide and supervise subordinates. This function carries out the objectives established in planning. Basically, leading consists of supervision, motivation, and communication.

All employees need and expect to be supervised. This supervision may take a strict form with close supervision of employees, or it may be loose, low structured direction. Some jobs necessitate that employees be under constant surveillance. Other jobs are structured to allow the bare minimum of supervision, such as a weekly report sent to the boss 500 miles away. In between these two extremes are an infinite number of superior-subordinate supervisory relations. Supervision requires observation of the work, workers, and working conditions to assure the unit's objectives are achieved.

Leading additionally has motivating responsibilities. No matter how fine the plans or efficient the organization, nothing happens until the people who make up the organization are stimulated to perform. This stimulus may be totally internal to the employee, but most frequently it requires the leader to initiate and reinforce motivators. Early studies of management and human behavior stressed the motivating power of money. We now recognize that what effectively motivated in 1900 has little relevance to our current affluent society. Today, the more than 80 million members of the American workforce are better educated and more financially secure than any previous generation. Basic physiological, security, and association needs have been met through high pay, liberal fringe benefits, and attractive working conditions. Though these extrinsic variables are important, many workers seek more from their jobs. They desire to satisfy esteem and self-actualization needs in the workplace, and therefore they seek the intrinsic qualities of recognition, achievement, growth, and advancement from their work.

Those who lead must be able to effectively communicate with those he leads. Clearly, no manager can succeed unless he can express his ideas in a form that others can understand. A thorough review of the communication process is provided in Chapter 4, so we need only mention its importance here. Effective communication facilitates the initiation of work and keeps subordinates informed as to how they are performing, which are obviously important parts of the administrator's job.

EVALUATING

The final function an administrator performs is evaluation. This function reviews, regulates, and controls performance to insure it conforms to the standards set in the planning function. The evaluation process begins with performance standards established in planning. Performance is measured, compared to the standards, and should there be significant deviations, corrective actions are instituted. As with leadership, evaluation may be strict or loose. However, where the evaluation process is lax, we increase the probability of failing to note and correct errant activities.

Evaluation merges with the planning, organizing, and leading functions when action is initiated to correct deviant performance. If performance is found to be unsatisfactory, one option is to alter the plans; that is, adjusting the objectives, policies, or subplans. Deviations may not be so much a result of inadequate performance as it is a result of inadequate or incorrect plans. A second option is to reorganize. Altering the relationships between the activities to be performed, the personnel to perform them, and the physical factors necessary may correct the deviation. Finally, correction can be achieved through the leadership function. By increasing or decreasing the depth of supervision, altering motivators, or changing communication patterns, performance that is out of tolerance may be brought into line.

It is possible to evaluate performance activities in terms of quantity, quality, time, or cost criteria. However, given the demands upon the administrator, evaluating all possible activities under his responsibility is not possible. The effective administrator will therefore initiate strategic evaluation at points critical to the attainment of his unit's goals. In addition to these externally imposed evaluations, many managers have recently recognized the value of allowing employees to evaluate their own performance. The administrator who possesses confidence and trust in his employees, and who views them as honest, hard working, and desirous of assuming responsibilities, will relegate imposed evaluations to minor importance and encourage individuals to utilize self-evaluations. With self-evaluation, employees measure, compare, and correct their own actions, as they deem it necessary, so their contribution to the organizational unit's goals can be optimized.

SUMMARY

The purpose of this chapter has been to briefly survey the administrative process. The reader will find terms and concepts that were presented here reappearing throughout the following pages.

Our approach has been to review the functions that managers and administrators perform. Though the degree of emphasis may differ considerably at different levels in the organization, it is our contention all administrators perform each of the four functions.

We can now proceed to the subject of conflict—*what* it is and *why* it is important to the administrator.

2

An Interactionist Approach

The previous chapter discussed decision making as part of the planning function. This is a narrow perspective because decision making is a process that permeates the entire administrative framework and ties the four functions together. It is in decision making that we develop and select from alternatives the actions that will lead toward goal attainment. Though it is frequently discussed only in the planning function, decision making is also an integral part of organizing, leading, and evaluating. And, as the remainder of this section will explain, this vital decision-making activity has become increasingly more difficult to perform in today's pluralistic organizations.

Though administrators have never had an easy time in the decision-making process, it is more difficult today than in previous generations as a result of conflicting group goals and expectations. Opposition is seen as a way of life among members of both small and large groups—through interorganization and intraorganization conflict. We find special interest groups protecting their sacred territories by playing expected roles: a plant location decision by a manufacturing firm has management trying to resolve differences between such varied interest groups as union officials, stockholders, community organizations, and government bodies; or a university president's decision as to the feasibility of co-educational dormitories finds opposing positions among trustees, faculty, students, parents, and alumni. No matter how clear the evidence may be that a particular course should be taken, there are few decisions made today that receive unanimous support.

The vast majority of administrative decisions are more difficult to make and there are no indications that this difficulty will decrease during the coming decades. Therefore it appears that between and among individuals, groups, and organizations, *pluralism* is a fact of life.

PHILOSOPHIES OF CONFLICT

When we accept that unanimity does not exist in complex organizations, we acknowledge that friction is part of the administrator's job. Katz and Kahn [1] perceive this adjudicating of conflicting demands to be one of the main functions of top management, while Gross [2] refers to friction as the factor that differentiates the real administrator from an administrator on paper. Just as decision making comprehensively permeates planning, organizing, leading, and evaluating, managing conflict is an overriding concept that pervades the four basic functions. Disappointingly, this view of conflict management is not widespread. Only recently have the ideas expressed by Katz and Kahn or Gross gained acceptance among students of conflict.

It is possible to differentiate three philosophies that reflect managerial attitudes toward conflict, arbitrarily labeled for our discussion as traditional, behavioral, and interactionist. The first two are descriptive because they represent predominant views espoused in the management literature. The third is normative, demonstrating what this writer believes should be management's direction today. Further, the material in the later chapters of this book grow out of the interactionist philosophy.

The prescription of the early management theorists, the traditionalists, towards conflict was simple. It should be eliminated. *All* conflicts were seen as destructive and it was management's role to rid the organization of them. This philosophy dominated the management literature during the late nineteenth century and continued to the middle 1940s.[3]

This traditional philosophy was followed by the behavioral view, which unfortunately is still the generally accepted approach to managing

---

[1] Daniel Katz and Robert L. Kahn, *The Social Psychology of Organizations* (New York: John Wiley and Sons, 1966).

[2] Bertram M. Gross, *The Managing of Organizations* (New York: Free Press of Glencoe, 1964).

[3] A significant exception is the work of Mary Parker Follett. She was cognizant of the value of constructive conflict in the 1920s. Her strong behavioral orientation placed her a quarter of a century ahead of her time.

conflict in the majority of organizations. The behavioralists' philosophy can best be described as "acceptance" of conflict. They have accurately perceived that complex organizations, by their very nature, have built-in conflicts. Disagreements over goals clearly exist. Sections compete for recognition. Departments compete for prestige. Other groups compete to increase their boundaries. All compete for power.

The behavioralists' view of conflict seeks to rationalize its existence. Typical of this pervasive attitude is Katz: [4] ". . . it should be added that we are not assuming that all conflict is bad and that the only objective toward which we should work is the resolution of conflict. Group conflict has positive social functions. . ." Or Bennis' comment that

> We do not believe that the elimination of conflict is invariable or even typically the desirable goal in wise management of conflict as many who identify consensus with agreement tend to do. Conflicts stem basically from differences among persons and groups. Elimination of conflict would mean the elimination of such differences. The goal of conflict management is, for us, better conceived as the acceptance and enhancement of differences among persons and groups. . . .[5]

Attitudes toward conflict such as these, though they recognize that conflict is inherent, give it only superficial acceptance. They grasp for supportive material to defend conflict's existence. Though encouragement of conflict is occasionally alluded to, such as Bennis' mention of "enhancement," nowhere is there found the active seeking of conflict or the positive creation of the conditions that breed conflict.

The behavioralists, in their efforts to "build a case" for conflict, are rationalizing: sure we have conflict, but it's good for the organization. When they think in terms of "managing" conflict, they demonstrate their uncertainty in its positive value by engrossing themselves entirely in the development of conflict resolution techniques. If conflict is truly of value to an organization, a more positive approach is needed.

The third philosophical stage is the positive approach. The interactionist philosophy differs from the behavioral in that it

1. recognizes the absolute necessity of conflict,
2. explicitly encourages opposition,
3. defines conflict management to include stimulation as well as resolution methods, and

[4] Chapter 9, "Approaches to Managing Conflict," by Daniel Katz, in *Power and Conflict in Organizations,* edited by Robert L. Kahn, and Elise Boulding, © 1964 by the Foundation on Human Behavior, Basic Books, Inc., Publishers, New York.

[5] Warren G. Bennis, Kenneth D. Benne, and Robert Chin, eds., *The Planning of Change* (2nd ed.) (New York: Holt, Rinehart and Winston, Inc., 1969), p. 152.

4. considers the management of conflict as a major responsibility of all administrators.

A review of current managerial practice finds few administrators employing the interactionist philosophy of conflict management. We appear to have made little progress since Ephron's comment in 1961 that "in so far as administrators have been troubled by conflict within their organizations, they have sought not so much to understand its origins as to find ways of reducing it." [6] Hopefully, once the reader has completed this book he will better *understand* conflict from the interactionist perspective.

VALUE OF CONFLICT

The interactionists readily accept and encourage conflict. They have expanded the term "conflict management" through recognition that it is a two-sided coin. They acknowledge that few have recognized its stimulation counterpart whereas much has been made of the resolution side. The interactionist believes that just as the level of conflict may be too high and require a reduction, it is also often too low and in need of increased intensity. The interactionists believe organizations that do not stimulate conflict increase the probability of stagnant thinking, inadequate decisions, and at the extreme, organizational demise. Additionally, they find some strong evidence to support their claims. Hall and Williams [7] conclude ". . . established groups tended to improve more when there was conflict among members than when there was fairly close agreement. . . ." They observed that when groups were formed to further analyze decisions that had been made by individuals, the average improvement by groups that exhibited high conflict was 73 percent greater than in those characterized by low conflict conditions. Several relevant real-life examples will dramatize the results from inadequately low levels of conflict.

The bankruptcy of the Penn Central Railroad has been generally attributed to mismanagement and a failure of the firm's board of directors to question actions taken by management.[8] The board was composed of outside directors, who met monthly to oversee the railroad's operations. Few questioned the decisions made by the operating management, though there was evidence that several board members were uncomfortable with

[6] Lawrence R. Ephron, "Group Conflict in Organizations: A Critical Appraisal of Recent Theories," *Berkeley Journal of Sociology,* Spring, 1961, p. 53.

[7] Jay Hall and Martha S. Williams, "A Comparison of Decision-Making Performances in Established and Ad Hoc Groups," *Journal of Personality and Social Psychology,* February, 1966, p. 217.

[8] Peter Binzen and Joseph R. Daughen, *Wreck of the Penn Central* (Boston: Little, Brown & Co., 1971).

many major decisions made by the management. Apathy and a desire to avoid friction allowed poor decisions to stand unquestioned. The value to the Penn Central of an inquiring and demanding board, which sought to force management to discuss and justify key decisions and the alternatives from which they were selected, can only be postulated.

Assael's study of conflict between manufacturers and dealers in the automobile industry [9] demonstrated Studebaker to be largely conflict free. One writer's [10] analysis of Assael's findings underscores the relationship between conflict and organizational success: "Perhaps more conflict between Studebaker and its dealers and employees might have saved the organization."

Reports on top level discussions in the early 1960s concerning America's role in Vietnam indicate that those individuals who privately questioned the views of the majority of the Presidential advisors refrained from openly questioning some obviously weak assumptions and poor logic. The environment created by both Presidents Kennedy and Johnson was not one to support minority disagreement.[11] As with the Penn Central debacle, it can only be postulated how decisions might have differed had conflict been encouraged.

As the above examples indicate, complex organizations may be in need of techniques for stimulation far more frequently than they require techniques for resolution. Constructive conflict is both valuable and necessary. Without conflict, there would be few new challenges; there would be no stimulation to think through ideas; organizations would be only apathetic and stagnant. Rico [12] further elaborates that "the absence of conflict may indicate autocracy, uniformity, stagnation, and mental fixity; the presence of conflict may be indicative of democracy, diversity, growth and self-actualization." Conflict is *the* vital seed from which growth and success germinate.

SURVIVAL REQUIRES CHANGE

There are but few things we can predict with certainty. One of these is that changes will occur. A major responsibility of an administrator is to guide his organizational unit in reacting to change. External factors in

[9] Henry Assael, "Constructive Role of Interorganizational Conflict," *Administrative Science Quarterly*, Vol. 14, #4, December, 1969, pp. 573-82.

[10] Louis R. Pondy, "Varieties of Organizational Conflict," *Administrative Science Quarterly*, December, 1969, p. 503.

[11] Irving L. Janis, "Groupthink," *Psychology Today*, November, 1971, pp. 43-46 and 74-76.

[12] Leonard Rico, "Organizational Conflict: A Framework for Reappraisal," *Industrial Management Review*, Fall, 1964, p. 67.

society are dynamic in nature and those organizations that do not adapt will not survive. The truth of the Hegelian dialectic still appears to hold. Hegel recognized that all changes develop from conflict or through the clash of opposites. The interaction in this clash produces a new situation. Marx accepted the Hegelian doctrine when he postulated that for every thesis there existed an antithesis. Out of this confrontation develops a synthesis stronger than either the thesis or the antithesis. As will be demonstrated later in this section, this confrontation or conflict "is the root of personal and social change." [13]

The belief that conflict is both a source and result of change is not universally accepted. Most writers have recognized only that change brings about conflict: "Social change involves a redistribution of power and privilege; therefore, it will be resisted by some and sought by others; hence conflict." [14]

The interactionist philosophy acknowledges that change develops from dissatisfaction, from the desire for improvement and from creative development of alternatives. Changes do not just happen, but are inspired by conflict. Desegregation in the South is illustrative of conflict's role in change. Sherif [15] describes a 1965 study of desegregation decisions in ten of the largest cities in the southern United States. Changes were found to follow a pattern of crisis initiating from various forms of open conflict.

Another recent example demonstrates the impact conflict has had on altering the direction and role of higher education in America. The student-administration confrontations during the last half of the 1960s warrant recognition as a significant change stimulator. Out of these conflicts has come a concern for reduction of archaic traditions that were irrelevant to the learning process of the 1970s. Additionally, other conflicts between legislators, administrators, and faculty have resulted in greater awareness of the organization's objectives, accountability for its performance, and better utilization of the public and private resources allocated to higher education. Again, change does not just happen. It requires a seed—the seed of conflict!

PARADOX OF CONFLICT

The purpose of openly challenging ideas and philosophies is to force re-evaluation. Where we have an environment that supports conflict, per-

---

[13] Morton Deutsch, "Conflicts: Productive and Destructive," *Journal of Social Issues,* January, 1969, p. 19.

[14] Joe Kelly, *Organizational Behaviour* (Homewood, Ill.: Richard D. Irwin, Inc., 1969), p. 503.

[15] Muzafer Sherif, *In Common Predicament: Social Psychology of Intergroup Conflict and Cooperation* (Boston: Houghton-Mifflin Co., 1966), p. 103.

ceived differences can be discussed and analyzed. The additional thought, and discussion generated by conflict only acts to reinforce the merit of a position that is the strongest of the available alternatives. A paradox is created because tolerance of conflict is counter to most cultures in developed nations. The United States, Canadian, and advanced European cultures have successfully engendered in their inhabitants a "fear of conflict," and a desire for at least tacit agreement. Most organizations today reinforce this sentiment. Let us take a closer look at the sources of this philosophy.

The early years of our development are when we are most susceptible to influence. From the time we reach an age of understanding through the primary school years, we have been inculcated with the value of getting along with others and avoiding conflicts. The home, school, and church are the three major institutions that share the responsibility for reinforcing anticonflict values during the developing years of a child.

The home has historically reinforced the authority pattern through the parent figure. Parents knew what was right and children complied. Conflict between children or between parents and children has generally been actively discouraged. The traditional school systems in developed countries have reflected the structure of the home. Teachers had *the* answers and were not to be challenged. Disagreements at all levels were viewed negatively. The last major influencing institution, the church also has supported anticonflict values. Church doctrines, for the most part, advocate acceptance without questioning. The religious perspective emphasizes peace, harmony, and tranquility. This is best exemplified by the teachings of the Roman Catholic Church. According to its beliefs, the Pope's word on religious matters is infallible. Such dogma has discouraged questioning the teachings of the church.

In addition to the influence of the three institutions mentioned above, entire countries such as the United States have further fostered an anticonflict image by developing a national pride as a peace-loving nation. Multibillion dollar expenditures are made each year for defense, not offense. Preparation to fight is made only because others may initiate force and therefore protection is justified. If it is survival of the fittest, America will be prepared, although the striving for the attainment of peace dominates the thinking of the nation's people.

We are still operating under the influence of traditional philosophical teaching. Conflicts of any type or form are bad. The vast majority of us have been influenced at home, in school, and through the church to eliminate, suppress or avoid conflict. Further, it has made us uncomfortable to be in its presence. Abraham Maslow expressed this view vividly in describing our society as one where there generally exists ". . . a fear of conflict, of disagreement, of hostility, antagonism, enmity. There is much stress on getting along with other people, even if you don't like them." [16]

The term conflict has a negative connotation for many in our society. The semantic problem has resulted in viewing conflict only from a negative perspective—as destructive or annihilatory. As we already recognize, conflict has a positive side that is repressed in our culture. We are inculcated with anticonflict views from childhood, and as a result most of us grow up with mores sanctioning unquestioned authority. Disagreement is considered unacceptable; all conflicts are bad. Might makes right, and if not might, at least formal authority. Bergen and Haney [17] report an American Management Association study that supports our contention. An overwhelming majority of 200 managers agreed that the most important single skill of an executive is his ability to get along with people.

We live in a society that has been built upon anticonflict values. Parents in the home, teachers and administrators in schools, teachings of the church, and authority figures in social groups all traditionally reinforce the belief that disagreement breeds discontent, which acts to dissolve common ties, and eventually leads to destruction of the system. Certainly we should not be surprised that children raised to view all conflict as destructive will mature into adults who will maintain and encourage the same values.

While these traditional beliefs that all conflict is detrimental are erroneous, we still find few indications that those who administer complex organizations are becoming tolerant of disagreement. Some organizations have established mechanisms to handle friction,[18] but they are by far in the minority.

Too few administrators accept, and almost none attempt to stimulate, conflict. It is true that conflict is uncomfortable and that it can be a source of problems. But additionally true, and this is what is paramount to the administrator, conflict is absolutely necessary in organizations if they are to maintain their viability and to increase the probability of their surviving. One may speculate that the reason administrators are paid the highest salaries in organizations is to compensate for their supposed acceptance of conflict. A good part of their remuneration may be viewed as "combat pay" to work in an environment that is, and must be, constantly uncomfortable.

The predominant view of conflict held by most individuals and groups

---

[16] Abraham Maslow, *Eupsychian Management* (Homewood, Ill.: Richard D. Irwin, Inc., 1965), p. 185.

[17] Garret L. Bergen and William V. Haney, *Organizational Relations and Management Action* (New York: McGraw-Hill Book Company, 1966).

[18] Note the increase in the number of organizations that have created the position of Ombudsman, to act as a conflict resolver.

is demonstrated in an enlightening study presented by Elise Boulding [19] illustrating the extent to which anticonflict sentiments permeate our society. Series of groups were formed to study a problem, some containing a deviant, who challenged and questioned dominant positions; others without. As we might expect, in every case, the group containing a deviant developed a richer analysis of the problem and a more elegant solution. When each group was then asked to drop one member, in every group that had a deviant member, it was he who was ousted. When given the opportunity, the childhood socialization that conflict was undesirable arose and the confronting force was eliminated, irrespective of its positive value. Our desire for consensus and agreement influences us more than the desire for effective performance.

Because individuals are products of their culture, we should not be surprised to find that antidisagreement values dominate the literature; scholars in the administrative discipline are enamoured with the idea of a smoothly operating enterprise. They see the administrator as the great resolver of disagreement. It should also not be surprising to find little effort expended on a comprehensive study of conflict management. Rather, the overriding desire for peace and tranquility within organizations has resulted in confusing the study of conflict resolution with conflict management.

The "great peacemakers" have made a weak basic assumption. They accept the notion that since conflict does exist in organizations, it *must* be in excess of the level that is desired. They assume it is the administrator's role to reduce tensions. Their conclusion then is to initiate actions to reduce conflict. But the goal of management is not harmony and cooperation—it is effective goal attainment! Elimination of conflict is not realistic in complex organizations, nor would such elimination be desirable. As Rico has noted, "the individuals or groups who are most vocal in advocating 'harmony and happiness' in an environment devoid of conflict, may only be protecting their vested interests in the *status quo*." [20]

It seems entirely likely that many, if not most, organizations need more conflict, not less. More organizations are dying from complacency and apathy than are dying from an overabundance of conflict. The unsuccessful have failed to perceive alterations in society's values, in the community, and in their employees. Organizations must therefore adapt to the rapid changes in their environment, and this requires change. Those administrators who naively succeed in eliminating conflict dramatically increase the probability that their organization will not survive.

[19] Elise Boulding, "Further Reflections on Conflict Management," in Kahn and Boulding's text *Power and Conflict in Organizations* (New York: Basic Books, Inc., 1964), pp. 147-48.

[20] Leonard Rico, "Organizational Conflict: A Framework for Reappraisal," *Industrial Management Review*, Fall, 1964, p. 67.

SUMMARY

Three philosophies describe the progression of conflict thought: traditional, which sought elimination of all conflict; behavioral, which accepted it; and interactionist, which actively encourages conflict. It is the interactionist perspective that becomes the framework for the remaining chapters.

Managing conflict is the nucleus of successful administration. An organization and its administrators must be primarily concerned with survival, which can only result from adaptive change. Because change is an output of conflict, an understanding of conflict should be a significant part of the study of administration and organizations.

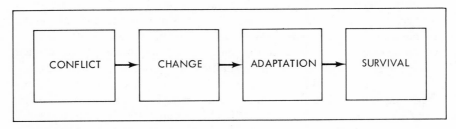

FIGURE 2–1   CONFLICT-SURVIVAL MODEL

The conflict management process is not executed easily. Planning and evaluating conflict intensity makes administration one of the most difficult professions. Each administrator is responsible for creating an environment that supports conflict and allows for appreciation of differences. Further, he needs to understand that conflict management is not merely conflict resolution, but stimulation as well. He knows that it is only by chance that conflict levels are that which he seeks.

Figure 2–2 depicts the challenge of administration—balancing the conflict fulcrum by utilizing resolution and stimulation tools. At the balancing point, effective (E_1) attainment of goals exists, along with efficient (E_2) utilization of resources. This challenge is met through setting conflict standards and development of evaluative controls to allow the organization to proceed toward its true potential.

The following chapter will be concerned with terminology. Emphasis will be placed on clarifying semantic ambiguities surrounding conflict, competition, and cooperation. Part II seeks to review sources of conflict, followed in Part III with methods of resolving and creating opposition.

FIGURE 2–2   CHALLENGE OF ADMINISTRATION

Part IV will develop conflict's application through a conflict management model. The final part of this volume will allow the reader to directly apply his knowedge through cases and conflict exercises.

3

A Point

of Departure

Conflict is a term that has acquired a multitude of meanings. Much of the semantic jungle has been created by the number of disciplines including anthropology, economics, political science, psychiatry, psychology, sociology, and management who are concerned with conflict. Further, the term has a preconceived meaning to most individuals whose value systems strongly influence their interpretations of conflict. Unlike many other words, conflict holds strong negative connotations to many, is neutral to some, and viewed positively by others.

"Conflict may connote animality, violence, destruction, barbarization, loss of civilized control, irrationality. Alternatively, conflict may connote adventure, novelty, clarification, creation, growth, dialectical rationality." [1]

The negative connotations with which many view the term result from reference to overt action. For example, when reference is made to the Arab-Israeli conflict, few individuals respond in a positive manner. A more normal response is concern over troublesome fighting, alarm at one nation's attempt to annihilate the other, and the desire to resolve the conflict that exists. Clearly, conflict of this type is viewed in negative terms, and correctly so. But, conflict has a vital positive side. When the Israelis'

[1] Warren G. Bennis, Kenneth D. Benne, and Robert Chin, eds., *The Planning of Change* (2nd ed.) (New York: Holt, Rinehart and Winston, Inc., 1969), p. 150.

Assistant Minister of Defense questions the Minister's strategy for logistic support at the front line, conflict also exists. Here, conflict *supports* the overall objective of the Minister's office, through questioning and rethinking of a particular decision. Conflict, therefore, describes a broad range of actions. It ranges from a minimum level of doubt, up through and including the extreme of annihilating the opponent. But such a description is too broad and, hence, inadequate for our use. Clearly, we need a tighter definition if we are to better understand the subject.

DEFINITION

Conflict, as the term will be used throughout this book, refers to all kinds of opposition or antagonistic interaction. It is based on scarcity of power, resources or social position, and differing value structures. Fink [2] views it as comprising two forms: (1) antagonistic psychological relations, and (2) antagonistic interaction. He differentiates the two by describing the former in terms of incompatible goals, mutually exclusive interests, emotional hostility, and differing value structures. Antagonistic interactions are overt; they can range from subtle, indirect and highly controlled forms of interference to direct, violent and uncontrolled struggle. Our definition covers the extremes from latent conflict, whether issues are formulated or not, to overt acts including strikes, riots, and war.

The above definition is purposely broad. It does not assume that inherent incompatibilities must exist in the situation. Subtle interferences need not require basic incompatibilities. Further, our definition does not assume overt struggle. Some writers require signs of manifest fighting as criteria for existence of conflict, but this obviously is only a part of the concept of conflict. If we assume that overt struggle is necessary in any conflict, we have adversely and negatively influenced the reaction to the concept. Any action that requires open struggle is in almost all cases undesirable, and results in clouding and misconstruing the idea and value of conflict.

An additional requirement of our definition is awareness. For an administrator to study conflict, it is necessary that he perceive it. Some theoreticians might find this constraint too limiting, but it appears necessary for the practitioner. It is necessary to appraise situations as they are seen; recognizing, of course, that conflicts perceived may not be real while many actual conflicts may not be perceived. When two doctors cannot agree on the correct diagnosis of a mutual patient, it becomes irrelevant that they

[2] Clinton F. Fink, "Some Conceptual Difficulties in the Theory of Social Conflict," *Journal of Conflict Resolution*, December, 1968, pp. 412-60.

in fact are both saying the same thing. If one talks about a psychological problem and the other a physiological problem, though each recognizes it as initiating from mental strain, a conflict exists. In truth, there may be no conflict; but for our purposes, if one is perceived then it exists. It may be easily ajudicated through problem-solving on the semantic difference, but in our terms such a perceived difference is a conflict.

The conflict we are describing is a social phenomenon, and is made up interpersonal, intergroup, and intragroup interactions. These three types of conflict consist of interactions between two or more persons, two or more groups, and between individuals in the same group. It excludes conflict as the term is used in psychology or psychiatry. In those disciplines, the term means internal human conflict—conflict within the individual. Role conflict, for example, is not relevant to this study, except in the impact that conflict has upon social interaction and group goal attainment. Our analysis will concern itself with the sociological view of interpersonal, intergroup, and intragroup interactions, and exclude the psychological ramifications, except where they may have impact on the social framework.

FUNCTIONAL VERSUS DYSFUNCTIONAL

Although, to this point, we have made a strong argument in favor of conflict in organizations, clearly we do not and cannot advocate all types or intensities of conflict. Some support the goals of the organization and improve performance; these are functional, constructive forms of conflict. Additionally, there are those that hinder organizational performance; these are dysfunctional or destructive forms.

A major thesis of this book is that conflict has significant value to any organization. Concern has been expressed about the need to rid organizations of "peacemakers" who have traditionally sought to abolish all forms of conflict. We now must qualify our analysis by differentiating between those forms that are functional and those that are not. The former represents confrontation that benefits or supports the goals of the organization. Any conflict that cannot meet this standard is undesirable and the administrator should seek its eradication. The demarcation between functional and dysfunctional is neither clear nor precise. No level of conflict can be adopted at face value as acceptable or unacceptable. We will find that the level that creates healthy and positive involvement towards one group's goals, may in another group or in the same group at another time, be highly dysfunctional, requiring immediate conciliatory attention by the administrator.

A final point is needed on the two types of conflict before we leave the topic. Our differentiation between functional and dysfunctional has been in terms of organizational performance. Some administrators inadvertently err by determining a conflict's constructiveness relative to the participants involved. In terms of functional or dysfunctional value, it is irrelevant how the participants perceive the conflict. The participants may perceive an action as dysfunctional, in that the outcome is personally dissatisfying to them. In our framework, it would be functional if it furthers the objectives of the organization.

If Professors Jones and Smith, at the local university, each desire a promotion from associate professor to full professor next year, but only one will be selected, they may view this conflict as dysfunctional. They are each busy improving their classroom teaching, expanding their participation on university committees, and burning the midnight oil in order to increase the number of their publications, while at the same time getting an ulcer from this pressure—all due to the desire for that promotion. The result, in terms of the organization, is extremely functional. Two faculty members are excelling. They are improving the offering they give to their students, are aiding and improving the internal functioning of the university, and are increasing the academic recognition of the school through publication. Now if you should ask our Professors Smith or Jones if they think this conflict and competition resulting from a scarce resource (one promotion slot) is functional or dysfunctional, they might rightly see it as the latter on a personal level. But an administrator is concerned with total performance of his group or organization. This example has resulted in improved organization performance and would be a functional conflict.

COMPETITION

Our example of Professors Smith and Jones' effort to achieve a promotion was an example not only of conflict, but also of competition. There existed rivalry between two or more parties to gain advantage over another person or group, but not with the ultimate aim of annihilating the rival. Can we then say that all competitions are conflicts or that all conflicts are competition? The terms are frequently used as synonyms for each other, which is erroneous. There is a difference. ⁓

If all competitions were conflicts, we would be saying that all rivalries involved a form of opposition. Clearly, we can cite numerous examples in which this requirement is not met. There need be no opposition or antagonistic interaction when two departments compete for the monthly performance award. Is there antagonism among the five supermarket chains in an urban area who each seek to get the highest percentage of employee subscribers to the United Fund? Need there be opposition between school districts in a region competing for top honors in nation-wide performance reviews? When battalions compete among themselves in various performance categories for specific honors or recognition, must there be conflict? The answer to these questions is no: there *can* be, but there need not be conflict.

When we look at the other relationship, we again find exceptions. If all conflicts included competition, we would be stating that rivalry existed in all antagonistic interactions. In many cases this is probably correct, but not all conflicts have one party seeking to gain advantage over another. The military officer who after presenting a proposal asks his staff to look it over for loopholes and inconsistencies is encouraging conflict, but there is no reason to believe that either the officer or the staff have gained advantage from this conflict supporting environment.

Figure 3–1 describes the relationship between these two concepts. We have conflicts that do not involve competition, we have competition that does not involve conflict, and we have an area of overlap where they are synonymous. Interestingly, there is a frequent cause-effect relationship be-

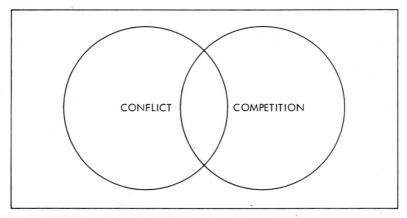

FIGURE 3–1   CONFLICT-COMPETITION RELATIONSHIP

tween the two. Intense competition can lead to conflict. We can expect this to occur when competition is based on scarcity of a resource—where one gains at another's expense. Our Professors Smith and Jones episode began in competition and resulted in conflict. If three fire station units are competing for the number one performance rating, the scarceness created by the availability of only one top position can result in conflict.

Where resources can expand, we need not expect conflict to develop.

Volkswagen, Toyota, Datsun, Fiat, Opel, and numerous other foreign automobile importers were able to compete throughout the 1960s without conflict developing because the market was expanding. When the market stagnated in the early 1970s, attempt to gain advantage over the competition
resulted in antagonistic opposition developing among the manufacturers,
distributors, and retailers as they sought to take sales from each other. As
long as the base was expanding, *each* could compete and gain, but when the
base no longer grew, one organization's gain was at the cost of one or more
of its rivals.

COOPERATION

Conflict's relationship with cooperation is considerably clearer, but surpris-
ingly as misunderstood as the relationship with competition. Many practitioners perceive cooperation as being the opposite of conflict. They have
traditionally sought the former and attempted to eliminate the latter. As
Figure 3–2 depicts, the two concepts exist on separate continuums. The

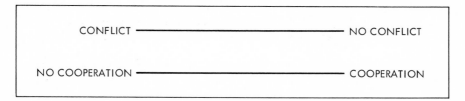

FIGURE 3–2   CONFLICT-COOPERATION RELATIONSHIP

opposite of conflict is no conflict and the opposite of cooperation is no cooperation. The strength of this view becomes clear when it is emphasized
that the elimination of conflict does not assure cooperation, nor does the
loss of cooperation imply the occurrence of conflict. As will be demonstrated in Chapters 7 and 8, attempts to reduce conflict utilize techniques
that increase cooperation, but the elimination of one does not create the
other. Whereas cooperation, which we define as working together toward
mutual goals, is frequently mentioned as a quality that organizations must
have, it will become clear as the reader progresses through the following
chapters, that cooperation can exist to too great an extent. Gross [3] has
directed attention to, and has been critical of, those placing extensive em-

[3] Bertram Gross, *The Managing of Organizations* (New York: Free Press of
Glencoe, 1964), p. 266.

phasis on cooperation due to its association with stability and routinization. When cooperation exists to the extent of absence of conflict, it is usually associated with avoidance of change and the continuation of outmoded forms of action. Therefore, we can literally conceive of an organization cooperating itself to death. The conceptual view shown in Figure 3–2 demonstrates that cooperation and conflict can exist together.

SUMMARY

This chapter defined conflict as opposition or antagonistic interaction, which can be dichotomized into functional and dysfunctional segments. The conflict that is functional and therefore leads to goal attainment should be encouraged, while the administrator should seek to eliminate all dysfunctional forms. Additionally, competition, which is frequently used interchangeably with conflict by practicing managers, was found to be similar to, but not always synonymous with conflict. Further, conflict and cooperation were described as two separate concepts that co-exist in an organization.

We should now have the background to proceed into an analysis of what causes conflict. The next section will introduce the reader into its three major sources: communication, structure, and personal-behavior factors.

II

SOURCES
OF CONFLICT

Any attempt by an administrator to alter a specific conflict position requires that he be knowledgeable of its origin. An understanding of the source improves the probability that the proper resolution or stimulation technique will be selected.

Conflict has varying causes that can be generally separated into three categories: communication, structure, and personal-behavior factors. The communicative source represents those disputes arising from semantic difficulties, misunderstandings, and noise in the communication channels. A misunderstanding over the term "quality education" illustrates one derivation of conflict. The concerned residents of a southern community expressed strong support for quality in their educational system. Both the school board and superintendent advocated "quality education," but differed bitterly on the interpretation of the desired result. The reason was simply that the term meant completely different things to each of the parties.

Structural conflict refers to opposition that develops from organizational roles and to barriers developed by management in their attempt to separate and coordinate activities. This source explains, for example, the conflict between union stewards and first-line management resulting from conflicting formal role expectations. It also explains the infamous conflicts between line and staff personnel.

Personal-behavior factors include individual idiosyncrasies and differing personal value systems. Reluctance of whites to accept integration with blacks is a conflict seeded in values, and any attempt to change the level of this conflict must include recognition of the source of the hostility. Solutions that will have success with one form of conflict may be totally inappropriate and unsuccessful when applied to a conflict derived from another source.

In the next three chapters several dozen empirical and philosophical studies that have sought to determine particular sources or causes of conflict, as well as theoretical examinations of the communications process in organizations, will be investigated. It will be the purpose of these chapters to search the studies and evaluate the impact of communications, structure, and personal-behavior factors as sources of conflict.

4

Communications

Much of the work in conflict resolution advocates improved communications to resolve social conflict. In discussions with practicing administrators, we found the most frequently mentioned source of conflict to be poor communications. Although poor communication is a simplified interpretation, it is a reasonable conclusion when we acknowledge that the average American spends nearly 70 percent of his waking hours communicating through writing, reading, speaking, and listening.

The source of *all* conflicts is certainly not poor communication, but there is considerable evidence to suggest that problems in the communication process act to retard collaboration and stimulate misunderstanding. Though not the sole source of conflict, communication is a major cause and the subject of this chapter.

The process of communication is the dynamic transmission of meaning from one person to another. For it to be successful, the information must not only be imparted, but it must be understood. Accordingly, the speaker who is not heard or the writer who is not read, does not communicate. Only when one is understood has communication taken place.

Perfect communication exists when a thought or idea is transmitted so that the mental picture perceived by the receiver is exactly what is envisioned by the sender. Though elementary in theory, perfect communication is never achieved in practice, for reasons we shall expand upon later in this section.

Rhenman [1] describes conflicts that result from the unsuccessful exchange of information as "pseudo-conflicts," to differentiate them from those based on substantive differences. He has developed a model, depicted in Figure 4–1, that delineates three specific causes of pseudo-conflicts: se-

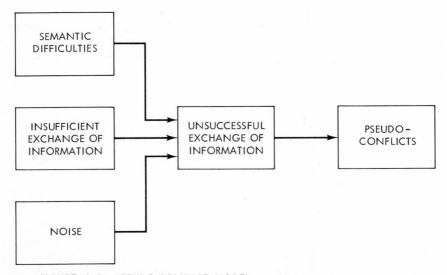

FIGURE 4–1   PSEUDO-CONFLICT MODEL

Source: Rhenman, Stromberg, and Westerlund, *Conflict and Cooperation in Business Organizations* (London: Wiley-Interscience, 1970), p. 68.

mantic difficulties, insufficient exchange of information, and noise.

Rhenman describes semantic difficulties as those that evolve from inaccessability to a common language or lack of available means of translation. He recognizes that information can only be translated through symbols, which are not the reality being discussed but abstract representations of that reality. Where no common pool of symbols exists, semantic difficulties can arise.

Second, the *insufficient* exchange of information is a source of pseudo-conflicts. When we recognize that the ability of the human machine to send and receive information is constrained by the imperfection of its communi-

---

[1] Eric Rhenman, Lennart Stromberg, and Gunnar Westerlund, *Conflict and Cooperation in Business Organizations* (London: Wiley-Interscience, 1970), pp. 67-69.

cation system itself, we cannot be surprised that the result is frequently less than what is desired.

Finally, Rhenman describes noise as a pseudo-conflict stimulant. Noise is any distortion of the signal quality. Such a distortion can be compared to the static disturbance occurring in a television set. This noise increases the difficulty of transmitting a distortion-free message. Hence, a message that may be accurate and comprehensible at the time it leaves the sender, can be distorted by noise in the communication channel. Included in the scope of Rhenman's definition of noise are mistakes on the part of the sender and listener weaknesses (i.e., saying you saw something when in fact you were in error, or the student thinking of tonight's party instead of the lecture he is currently attending).

COMMUNICATION MODEL

We can better expand on Rhenman's three sources of "pseudo-conflict" if we describe briefly a communication model.[2] A purpose, expressed as a message to be conveyed, is needed before communication can take place. It takes place between a source (the sender) and a receiver. The message is encoded (conversion of an idea or thought to symbolic form), passed by way of some medium (channel) to the receiver who retranslates (decodes) the message initiated by the sender. The result is a transference of meaning from one person to another.

This communication model is made up of six parts: (1) the communication source, (2) encoder, (3) message, (4) channel, (5) decoder. and (6) the communication receiver. Each of these parts affords opportunities for distortion of the communique.

Berlo describes four conditions that will affect the encoded message: skill, attitudes, knowledge, and the social-cultural system. An author's success in communicating to you is dependent on his writing skills, while his total communicative success includes his speaking, reading, listening, and reasoning skills as well. As with the writing of a book, if the author is without the requisite skills, his message will not reach you in the form desired. Each of us is aware that our attitudes greatly influence our behavior. We hold predisposed ideas on numerous topics and our communications are affected by these attitudes. Further, we are restricted in our communicative activity by the extent of our knowledge on the particular topic. We cannot

[2] David K. Berlo, *The Process of Communication* (New York: Holt, Rinehart, and Winston, 1960), pp. 30-32.

communicate what we do not know; and should our knowledge be too extensive, it is possible our receiver will not understand our message. Clearly, the amount of knowledge the source holds about his subject will affect the message he seeks to transfer. And finally, just as attitudes influence our behavior, so does our position in the social-cultural system in which we exist. Your beliefs and values, all part of your culture, act to influence you as a communicative source.

The message itself can cause distortion in the communicative process, regardless of the supporting apparatus used to convey it. Our message is the actual physical product from the source-encoder. "When we speak, the speech is the message. When we write, the writing is the message. When we paint, the picture is the message. When we gesture, the movements of our arms, the expressions on our face are the message." [3] Our message is affected by the code or the group of symbols we use to transfer meaning, the content of the message itself, and the decisions that the source makes in selecting and arranging both codes and content. Each of these three segments can act to distort the message.

The channel is the medium through which the message travels. It is selected by the source who must determine which channel will most effectively transfer his message. It is the selection of this mechanism that will bridge the gap between the source and the receiver. The most distinct classification of channels is formal and informal. Formal channels are established by the organization and transmit messages that relate to the professional activities of members. They traditionally follow the formal authority network within the organization. Other forms of messages, such as personal or social messages, will follow the informal channels within the organization.

The receiver is the object to whom our message is directed. But before he can receive, he must translate the symbols in the channel into a form he can understand—he must decode the message. Just as the encoder was limited by his skills, attitudes, knowledge, and social-cultural system, so is the receiver equally restricted. Just as the source must be skillful in writing or speaking, the receiver must be skillful in reading or listening. And both must be able to reason. One's level of knowledge will influence his ability to receive, as it did the source's ability to send. Finally, the receiver's predisposed attitudes and cultural background can act as distortions of the message being transferred.

This model of communication presented by Berlo, and the factors that create the unsuccessful exchange of information, as presented by Rhenman, clarify sources of communication distortion.

[3] *Ibid.*, p. 54.

SOURCES OF COMMUNICATION DISTORTION

When we analyze the communication model of Berlo and the pseudo-conflict model of Rhenman, we find that they are quite similar.

The semantic difficulties of Rhenman relate to Berlo's message. The insufficient exchange of information is comparable to the inadequacies that exist in the source, the receiver, and in the encoding and decoding processes. Finally, the noise described by Rhenman relates to distortions in Berlo's channel.

Strauss and Sayles summarize our findings in Figure 4–2 by noting specific barriers to communication. Distortions can develop at any point in the communication process. Conflict can develop as a result of insufficient

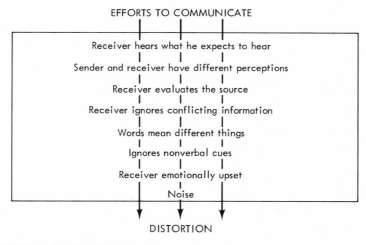

FIGURE 4–2 BARRIERS TO COMMUNICATION

Source: Leonard R. Sayles and George Strauss, *Human Behavior in Organizations* (Englewood Cliffs, New Jersey: Prentice-Hall, Inc., 1966), p. 256.

exchange of information, semantic difficulties in the message, or from noise in the communication channel.

A statement such as "I don't understand what you're saying," dramatizes what may result from the presence of any of the communicative barriers shown in Figure 4–2. It is also possible that the statement may actually mean the receiver did not agree with what was said.

Occasionally, an inadequate communique is recognized immediately. Responses from a receiver such as, "That contradicts what you told me yesterday," or "What you're asking is not clear to me," gives rapid feedback to the sender that there is a problem. More often, there is an absence of feedback, and the sender is never aware that effective communication has not taken place. It is only discovered later when the behavior of the receiver indicates lack of communication, or when the receiver states something approximating, "Oh, that's what you meant. . . ," or "I thought you meant. . . ."

As the above demonstrates, the key to successful communication is feedback. It indicates to the original sender whether his ideas have been received as they were originally intended. The feedback concept is as important in the transmission of written communication as it is in oral communication. Too often in the organizational setting, it is assumed that effective communication has taken place merely with the issuance of a written document: "Of course she must have known about the change in policy. We sent out a memo on it last month." The use of feedback improves the communication process and reduces the chance of major disparities between the thought or idea received and the one intended.

Given the brief review of communication theory and of the potential within the communication process for forming pseudo-conflict, a review of studies relating communication to conflict is indicated.

SEMANTIC DIFFICULTIES

Things mean different things to different people. This is particularly true with word connotations. When a individual is described as a "real winner," is it to be interpreted literally, or is it being said facetiously? "The meaning of words are *not* in the words, they are in *us*." [4] It is possible to find much support for the belief that semantic problems can impede communication essential for effective group performance. It has been reported that the difference in training of purchasing agents and engineers contributes to their conflict.[5] As with physicians and professional hospital administrators, their academic training and orientations differ significantly. Differences in training develops disparate terminology and jargon, which impedes the effective movement of ideas.

[4] S. I. Hayakawa, *Language in Thought and Action* (New York: Harcourt Brace Jovanovich, Inc., 1949), p 292.

[5] George Strauss, "Work-Flow Frictions, Interfunctional Rivalry, and Professionalism: A Case Study of Purchasing Agents," *Human Organization,* Summer, 1964, pp. 137-49.

Dearborn and Simon [6] performed a perceptual study having twenty-three business executives read a comprehensive case describing the organization and activities of a steel company. Six of the twenty-three executives were in the sales function, five in production, four in accounting, and eight in miscellaneous functions. Each manager was asked to write down the most important problem he found in the case. Eighty-three percent of the sales executives rated sales important, in contrast to 29 percent of the others. This, along with other results of the study, led the researchers to conclude that the participants perceived aspects in a situation that related specifically to the activities and goals of the unit to which they were attached. Clearly, a group's perception of organization actions is altered to align with the vested interest they represent. Such "selective perception" can be, and frequently is, a source of organizational conflict.

One researcher stated that the less differing units know about each other's job, the less collaboration will take place.[7] Further, this lack of knowledge can lead to unreasonable interunit demands. Animosities observed between a county welfare department and other county agencies in a southern California community were directly attributable to ignorance on the part of each agency as to the nature of duties of other agencies. In contrast to these interactions, smooth coordination and relations existed where nonwelfare agency members were familiar with the welfare department's responsibilities and contributions.

The above findings indicate not only that conflict can be stimulated by lack of understanding but also that lack of information generally can increase conflict.

AMBIGUITY VERSUS PERFECT KNOWLEDGE

If inadequate information or ambiguous information is a source of conflict, the existence of complete, perfect knowledge might be hypothesized as an environment where little or no conflict would exist. However, our research does not support this view.

Schelling [8] argues that perfect knowledge about another's options may impinge upon coordination. Ignorance forces the parties to agree on obvious alternatives, and perfect knowledge permits self-interest to undermine co-

[6] DeWitt C. Dearborn and Herbert A. Simon, "Selected Perception: A Note on the Departmental Identifications of Executives," *Sociometry,* June, 1958, pp. 140-44.

[7] E. J. Miller, "Technology, Territory, and Time," *Human Relations,* August, 1959, pp. 243-72.

[8] Thomas C. Schelling, *The Strategy of Conflict* (Cambridge: Harvard University Press, 1969).

operation. A more convincing argument is presented by Walton, Dutton, and Cafferty [9] who empirically researched the relationship between knowledge and conflict. Their study found that interdepartmental conflict increased when departments possessed more knowledge of each other's activities. Contrary to what might be intuitively expected, it may be concluded that too much knowledge of another unit's activities actually initiates conflict. Perfect knowledge reveals inequities, whereas imperfect knowledge diminishes disparities and makes coordination easier.

We would perceptively expect that ambiguity in communications would act to increase conflict. Most of the research supports this view. Kahn, Wolfe, et al.,[10] observed that ambiguity in the criteria used to evaluate the performance of a unit may create conflict. Another researcher found that uncertainty of the means to goal achievement increases the potential for interunit conflict.[11] Additionally, both Dalton,[12] and Dutton, and Walton [13] found that when there was difficulty in assigning credit or blame for performances between two departments, the probability of conflict developing between the two units was increased.

The above findings establish that inadequate, unclear, or ambiguous communications stimulate conflict. However, perfect knowledge or perfect communication does not improve coordination, but rather increases conflict. Therefore we find conflict being initiated when separate units have inadequate or ambiguous knowledge about one another, or to the other extreme where they hold perfect or complete knowledge.

CHANNELS

Our research indicates that the communication channels within the organization can significantly influence the level of conflict. March and Simon [14] reported that organizational channeling of information introduces bias into

9 Richard E. Walton, John M. Dutton, and Thomas P. Cafferty, "Organizational Context and Interdepartmental Conflict," *Administrative Science Quarterly,* December, 1969, pp. 522-42.

10 R. L. Kahn, D. M. Wolfe, R. P. Quinn, J. D. Snoek, and R. A. Rosenthal, *Organizational Stress: Studies in Role Conflict and Ambiguity* (New York: John Wiley and Sons, 1964).

11 Mayer N. Zald, "Power Balance and Staff Conflict in Correctional Institutions," *Administrative Science Quarterly,* June, 1962, pp. 22-49.

12 Melville Dalton, *Men Who Manage* (New York: John Wiley and Sons, 1959).

13 John M. Dutton and Richard E. Walton, "Interdepartmental Conflict and Cooperation: Two Contrasting Studies," *Human Organization,* Fall, 1966, pp. 207-20.

14 James G. March and Herbert A. Simon, *Organizations* (New York: John Wiley and Sons, 1958).

material that is communicated. They found that when information was passed between levels, it became altered as people interpreted "facts" differently. This presents serious problems for executives who, by definition, work through others and who depend upon their subordinates to interpret information and direct what they perceive to be the important facts upward through the organization's hierarchy. For example, the mayor of a large urban city cannot possibly know all the activities going on in the Recreation, Manpower, or Permits and Inspection Divisions of his city government. He depends on section supervisors, department managers, and division administrators to channel upward key information so the decisions he makes, which affect these divisions, will be of the highest quality. What section supervisors deem relevant will determine what is transmitted upward, which in turn will dramatically influence what the division managers receive. All along this chain, facts have been interpreted. Therefore, the information that finally reaches the mayor's office has been substantially filtered. What one manager perceives as superfluous, another may view as critical. Hence, the perceptions of subordinate administrators can restrict an accurate flow of information and initiate opposition.

Conflict can additionally be stimulated when communication channels deviate from the formal hierarchical structure. Lawrence and Lorsch [15] found support for this thesis when they observed that conflict could be initiated when there existed an inconsistency between the distribution of knowledge among groups and lateral influence patterns. Using the grapevine instead of formal authority lines or the skipping of authority levels when transmitting information through the scalar chain illustrate these forms of opposition initiators. The above observations lead us to conclude that conflict is stimulated by both the filtering process of communications when it passes between levels and by divergence of communications from formal authority lines.

SUMMARY

This chapter has sought to briefly discuss the communicative process, and to depict the possible areas of distortion that can develop and lead to conflict. Semantic difficulties, insufficient exchange of information, and noise in the communication channel are each barriers to communication and conflict sources.

Specific findings demonstrated semantic difficulties arise as a result of

[15] Paul R. Lawrence and Jay W. Lorsch, *Organization and Environment* (Boston: Division of Research, Graduate School of Business Administration, Harvard University, 1967).

differences in training, selective perception, and inadequate information about other units. The studies analyzed also demonstrated an interesting situation: conflict increases when either too little or too much communication takes place. Apparently an increase in communication is functional up to a point, whereupon it is possible to overcommunicate with a resultant increase in conflict. We may conclude that while an insufficient exchange of information and an abundance of information both increased conflict, a middle ground should be sought if one's objective is neither to increase or decrease conflict.

Finally, in this chapter we reviewed several studies that emphasized the impact the channel can play as a communication source. The studies substantiated that both the filtering process of communications between structural levels in the organization and divergence of communications from the formal authority-communication lines are stimulants to conflict.

5

Structure

Structural factors are defined as those variables in complex organizations that are, for the most part, controllable by executives within the organization. Though there is some overlapping between structure and the personal-behavior factors discussed in the following chapter, it is extremely important to separate the two. Structural factors are controllable and therefore amendable to the tools of the manager. Personal-behavior factors are those which organization members bring with them or are intrinsic in their jobs.

SIZE

Is the probability of conflict being initiated greater in larger organizations than in those with fewer members and less hierarchical levels? A review of several empirical studies can clarify this question.

A 1953 study of the Tennessee Valley Authority showed that conflict is likely to be greater in larger organizations.[1] The researcher sur-

[1] Phillip Selznick, *TVA and the Grass Roots* (Berkeley: University of California Press, 1953), p. 256.

mised that smaller organizations had narrower, clearer, and more specific establishment of means for attaining goals. When goals are more concise and well dispersed, opposition would be reduced. These conclusions were further supported by research undertaken in educational organizations.[2]

A positive correlation was found between three structural variables in conflicts between teachers and administrators. As schools increased in size, therefore requiring a larger number of authority levels, the number of conflicts and the rate of conflict intensity increased. The investigator observed that 83 percent of school systems having six or seven levels of authority evidenced high rates of disagreement, in contrast to only 14 percent of systems with three or fewer levels of authority. These significant results lend strong support for the expectation of higher conflict intensities within larger school organizations.

In contrast to the above findings, a comprehensive study of 250 separate organizational units from 6 organizations,[3] could not support the size-conflict relationship. While this more thorough investigation did not negate the findings of the previous researchers, it was possible to conclude that size of itself did not lead to serious conflict between echelons. The major disparity between this study and the others may be one of emphasis. Size may stimulate conflict, but its seriousness or intensity is certainly affected by other variables, which are frequently difficult to control under research conditions.

These studies would lead one to conclude that increased size, which results in more supervisory levels, does not reduce conflict and probably acts as a stimulant. We could postulate from these findings that the law enforcement organization of New York City, all other factors held constant, would be a more antagonistic environment than the neighboring force in Scarsdale. Size alone would restrict communication, impede interaction and foster separateness. Therefore, it can be generalized that as a structure increases in size, goals will become less clear, relationships will by necessity become more formal, specialization will create increased pressure to protect one's bailiwick, and more opportunities for distortion will occur as information must be passed through a greater number of levels. Each of these tendencies will impede a smooth and peaceful work environment.

[2] Ronald G. Corwin, "Patterns of Organizational Conflict," *Administrative Science Quarterly*, December, 1969, pp. 507-20.

[3] Clagett G. Smith, "A Comparative Analysis of Some Conditions and Consequences of Intra-Organizational Conflict," *Administrative Science Quarterly*, March, 1966, pp. 504-29.

BUREAUCRATIC QUALITIES

Routinization, specialization, and standardization are major factors contributing to the development of bureaucracies. Significant research has been undertaken into the impact these variables have upon conflict, though the findings are not clearly reconcilable.

One study [4] concluded that the likelihood of conflict was greater where there was less routinization in the design of jobs. As job structure is reduced, the probability of conflict would increase as the job becomes less programmed and surrounded by greater uncertainty. Lack of structure, in this case, heightens conflict intensity.

Another investigation was undertaken to determine if there was a correlation between conflict and specialization in school organizations.[5] Most of the correlations indicated a positive relationship, though only a few were statistically significant. Standardization, which was significantly correlated with conflict, dropped below statistical significance when controlled for the varying sizes of the schools studied.

Finally, one investigator has intuitively determined, after reviewing the relationship between organization design and conflict, that uniform tasks require a bureaucratic form of organization, whereas nonuniform tasks require a human-relations form.[6] Because most large scale organizations have both types of tasks and must seek to combine them, it was concluded that these contradictory forms act as a source of organization conflict.

The above studies have not clearly determined each of the bureaucratic qualities to be conflict stimulants. High degrees of specialization appear to be correlated with conflict, as is the need for both structure and viability in organization tasks. On the other hand, the evidence for standardized tasks as initiators is inconclusive.

Of particular interest is the apparent contradiction between two of the above findings. If increased specialization advances conflict levels, why does less job routine achieve the same end? Evidently, the division of labor increases boredom and fatigue, while a reduction in routine increases

---

[4] Phillip Selznick, *TVA and the Grass Roots* (Berkeley: University of California Press, 1953), p. 256.

[5] Ronald G. Corwin, "Patterns of Organizational Conflict," *Administrative Science Quarterly,* December, 1969, pp. 507-20.

[6] Eugene Litwak, "Models of Bureacracy Which Permit Conflict," *American Journal of Sociology,* September, 1961, pp. 177-84.

uncertainty. Jobs that are enlarged to increase the worker's interest and to capitalize on an individual's abilities, but that are highly programmed in terms of procedures, should not develop interpersonal hostilities as would the enlargement of job activities and an increased freedom from routine.

HETEROGENEITY OF STAFF

Tenure appears to be a relevant variable to be studied as a conflict source. One would hypothesize that as the tenure of group members increased, conflict would be less likely to develop. A study [7] conducted with established and ad hoc groups gives some support to this hypothesis. Established groups were shown to develop more constructive conflict than ad hoc formations. This would infer that groups which worked longer together, though experiencing conflict, had developed the functional variety; therefore improving overall group performance. This same investigation further found the major difference between the two forms of groups to be the direction of conflict. In established groups the attack was directed at the ideas presented by members, whereas in the ad hoc groups the individuals who presented the views were the object of attack.

In the school study previously cited,[8] a relationship was established between age of faculty members and degree of conflict. The results made evident that as the mean age of a faculty member increased, the incidence of conflict declined on nine of the researcher's ten measures. The conclusion drawn was that faculty members seem to become more peaceful as they grow older. If we can generalize from this study, it would lend support for stability among group members being a conflict reducing variable.

If it can further be assumed that length of employment with an organization and age are highly correlated, high turnover could be expected to stimulate conflict. This, in fact, is supported by the established/ ad hoc group study. Additionally, if increased age and tenure reduced conflict, and consequently change, the interactionist would support planned employee turnover and the purposeful inclusion of "young rebels" into groups to promote better adjustment to alterations in the environment and thus aid group performance effectiveness.

[7] Jay Hall and Martha A. Williams, "A Comparison of Decision-Making Performances in Established and Ad Hoc Groups," *Journal of Personality and Social Psychology,* February, 1966, pp. 214-22.

[8] Ronald G. Corwin, "Patterns of Organizational Conflict," *Administrative Science Quarterly,* December, 1969, pp. 507-20.

STYLE OF SUPERVISION

Supervisory style as a source of conflict has not been conclusively established, although the evidence suggests close styles of supervision as conflict initiators.

Rensis Likert,[9] former University of Michigan professor and supporter of democracy in organizations, strongly advocates general supervision and employee self-direction. He believes that a close, one-to-one supervisory style generally promotes more conflict among peers than does general supervision. Likert reasons that where employees can more directly plan and control their own work, structural and authority conflicts are reduced.

Likert's conclusions were not supported when supervisory style and conflict were studied in school organizations.[10] Though a positive correlation was found between close supervision and several conflict measures, with the total number of disputes significant, individually the number was not statistically significant.

PARTICIPATION

One form of supervisory style is to increase employee participation in the decision-making process. Behavioral scientists such as Likert, Douglas McGregor, Abraham Maslow, and Frederick Herzberg have made a substantial impact on current administrative teaching through their unrelenting support for increasing the democratic process in organizations. Given the impact of these scientists and their general support for reducing organizational conflict, one might intuitively hypothesize that joint decison making, where those who will be affected by a decision are made part of the decision-making body, would act to reduce conflict and promote cooperation. To the contrary, the literature does not support this hypothesis.

Several studies investigated involvement of teachers in the decision-making process and correlated their participation with conflict. One found participation and conflict to be positively correlated.[11] Another found that in decisions which affected the classroom situation, participation was

[9] Rensis Likert, *New Patterns of Management* (New York: McGraw-Hill Book Company, 1961).

[10] Ronald G. Corwin, "Patterns of Organizational Conflict," *Administrative Science Quarterly,* December, 1969, pp. 507-20.

[11] Donald I. Warren, "The Effects of Power Bases and Peer Group on Conformity in Formal Organizations," *Administrative Science Quarterly,* December, 1969, pp. 544-56.

positively related with the rate of disputes in nine out of ten items.[12] Only the number of "major incidents" was negatively correlated with participation. This latter study concluded this positive correlation occurred because the authority to make routine decisions permits a greater opportunity for the expression of existing disputes and allows more occasions for disagreements to arise. On the other hand, the opportunity to participate in the decision-making process might prevent minor irritations from developing into major incidents by providing occasions for individuals to express minor forms of conflict.

The comprehensive analysis of six organizations, mentioned earlier, also was an inquiry into the relationship between participation and conflict.[13] It was found that in highly structured organizations, where the need for joint decision making existed, there was a greater possibility of conflict developing. Further research [14] supports the findings of the previous studies by reinforcing the relationship between participation and conflict. These investigations found that where there was a lack of agreement over ultimate goals and values, forming a genuine conflict of interest, participation could act to intensify conflict.

The studies reviewed clearly depict an increase in conflict resulting from greater participation by organization members, especially where true value differences exist. Apparently, the high interaction incurred in participation only acts to solidify differences rather than facilitate coordination and cooperation. The result is greater differences of opinion and greater awareness of conflict. While the conflict intensity may, in reality, be no greater after participation than before, it tends to move the conflict from latent to overt.

REWARD SYSTEMS

In Chapter 6 the topic of goals will be discussed in some detail. But certainly as important as the ends to which effort is directed are the means used to achieve these ends.

The belief that reward systems can serve to either sharpen or blunt the latent or overt conflict that may exist within the organization was a

[12] Ronald G. Corwin, "Patterns of Organizational Conflict," *Administrative Science Quarterly,* December, 1969, pp. 507-20.

[13] Clagett G. Smith, "A Comparative Analysis of Some Conditions and Consequences of Intra-Organizational Conflict," *Administrative Science Quarterly,* March, 1966, pp. 504-29.

[14] See Mayer Zald, "Power Balance and Staff Conflict in Correctional Institutions," *Administrative Science Quarterly,* June, 1962, pp. 22-49, and George Strauss and Eliezer Rosenstein, "Workers Participation: A Critical View," *Industrial Relations,* February, 1970, pp. 197-214.

conclusion from a 1969 investigation.[15] The researchers developed a most logical thesis: the more the evaluations and rewards of higher management emphasize the separate performance of each department, rather than their combined performance, the greater the conflict. This thesis is supported through empirical research.

Conflict has been found to exist where different reward systems were provided for two or more groups, and where one's gain was at another's expense.[16] For example, the preference of production units for long, economical runs with its accompanying rewards, are in opposition to the rewards provided sales units from quick delivery to good customers. In this example, one unit is being rewarded for fewer runs that minimize costs, while the other unit is rewarded for speed, which frequently entails the need for a greater number of runs.

Line-staff conflicts can also be explained in terms of differing reward systems. Staff units value change, for this is the major way they justify their existence. This is in opposition to line units who value stability.[17] To line units, change has undesirable repercussions for their operations. Not only is change inconvenient but it also degrades current methods. Any change suggested by a staff unit implies the current methods are inadequate; an obviously degrading implication. The reward structure for line and staff units therefore often places the two groups in opposition to each other.

POWER

The ability to influence others includes the formal authority that the organization gives managers. This power may be a factor that influences the development of conflict. Several studies have been completed that expand our knowledge of the relevancy of power as a conflict source.

One study indicated power can facilitate coordination and concurrently reduce conflict.[18] Working in an academic environment, the researcher determined coordination was positively correlated with the principal of a school's reward, legitimate, referent, and even coercive power. Apparently, up to a certain level, increasing power improved co-

[15] Richard E. Walton and John M. Dutton, "The Management of Interdepartmental Conflict: A Model and Review," *Administrative Science Quarterly,* March, 1969, pp. 73-84.

[16] John M. Dutton and Richard E. Walton, "Interdepartmental Conflict and Cooperation: Two Contrasting Studies," *Human Organization,* Fall, 1966, pp. 207-21.

[17] Melville Dalton, *Men Who Manage* (New York: John Wiley and Sons, 1959).

[18] Donald I. Warren, "The Effects of Power Bases and Peer Group on Conformity in Formal Organizations," *Administrative Science Quarterly,* December, 1969, pp. 544-56.

ordination and therefore assisted in reducing conflict between the chief school administrator and his teaching staff.

Other investigations showed conflict arose when groups who were weak in power attempted to reallocate the power structure and force the powerful members to relinquish partial control.[19] Imbalances of organizational power by themselves may not initiate conflict, but when attempts are made to correct perceived inequities, hostility is apparently stimulated.

Finally, one investigator discerns a growing separation in modern organizations between ability and authority.[20] He describes the traditional structure as equating ability and authority: those with the most ability had positions of greatest authority. But in today's complex organizations an imbalance is developing which in turn festers conflict. Conflict is generated as those with authority find they are strongly dependent on those with expertise. Further, those with the expertise hold great informal authority because they can pass their knowledge to whom they wish, when they wish. This ability to withhold knowledge additionally increases their informal authority. Therefore, steep and heavily emphasized hierarchical differences in power cause lateral conflicts. These differences tend to emphasize individual power aspirations rather than increased horizontal coordination.

In summary, we conclude that low and moderate levels of power, made up of formal and informal authority, can assist in improving coordination and, therefore, work to reduce conflict. But where power is excessive, as perceived by a less powerful group, one may expect it to be challenged, causing increased conflict. Additionally, in modern organizations that utilize task, project, and matrix forms of organization, professionals whose expertise spells the success or failure of the unit hold considerable power. If this is not recognized, the result can be a considerable increase in opposition. This represents, in effect, a rapid development of traditional line-staff conflicts.

INTERDEPENDENCE

The final structural variable investigated is interdependence. Our research demonstrates interdependence to be a major source of organizational conflict.

[19] See Henry Assael, "Constructive Role of Interorganizational Conflict," *Administrative Science Quarterly,* December, 1969, pp. 573-82 and Cornelis J. Lammers, "Strikes and Mutinies: A Comparative Study of Organizational Conflicts Between Rulers and Ruled," *Administrative Science Quarterly,* December, 1969, pp. 558-72.

[20] Victor A. Thompson, *Modern Organization* (New York: Alfred A. Knopf, 1964).

When a pool of resources is relatively fixed, and when one group's gain is at the expense of another, increased conflict should be expected. A recent empirical investigation found conflict to increase where two or more units depend upon a common pool of scarce resources.[21]

This thesis was supported with research conducted with line-staff groups [22] and with purchasing agents.[23] The former found staff groups resented the asymmetries in their relationship with line groups. A one-sided situation existed. The staff was required to get along with the line, understand the line's problems, and justify their own existence; whereas none of these requirements was reciprocated by the line groups. Similarly, it was found that high dependence of purchasing agents on another group led them to make more concerted attempts to influence the terms of requisitions they received and therefore force two-way interaction.

Noted sociologist Georg Simmel,[24] after a thorough study of conflict, concurs with these findings: conflict will develop and expand where activities of one group are perceived to have fairly direct consequences on the ability of another to pursue its goals. Again, where one gains at another's expense, a zero-sum game, the seeds exist for expansion of conflict.

These findings lend strong evidence to the view that interdependence promotes conflict. Where we have one group gaining at another's expense or where asymmetrical (one-sided) interdependence exists, we can expect conflict to breed.

SUMMARY

This chapter has reviewed the major structural variables frequently believed to be sources of conflict in complex organizations. Our research seems to support the proposition that size acts as a positive force on conflict. The larger the organization, the greater the likelihood of conflict.

The bureaucratic factor of specialization was found to stimulate conflict. The organization's size may be the more critical variable because separating it from such characteristics as specialization and standardization is difficult.

Tenure and conflict were found to be inversely related. The potential

[21] John M. Dutton and Richard E. Walton, "Interdepartmental Conflict and Cooperation: Two Contrasting Studies," *Human Organization,* Fall, 1966, pp. 207-21.

[22] Melville Dalton, *Men Who Manage* (New York: John Wiley and Sons, 1959).

[23] George Strauss, "Work-Flow Frictions, Interfunctional Rivalry, and Professionalism: A Case Study of Purchasing Agents," *Human Organization,* Summer, 1964, pp. 137-49.

[24] George Simmel, *Conflict* (New York: Free Press of Glencoe, 1955).

for conflict seems to decrease with the increase in group member tenure. We have pointed out that this suggests conflict will be greatest where group members are younger and where turnover is high.

There is some indication that a close style of supervision increases conflict, but the evidence is not particularly strong. A result that was rather surprising, and contradictory to much current behavioral teaching, was that participation and conflict appear to be highly correlated. The evidence found in this chapter strongly suggests that those who have advocated more democracy in our complex organizations be made cognizant of indications that a high participative, democratic environment cannot, by itself, be expected to reduce social conflict between members.

Reward systems were found to create conflict where one unit's gain would be at another unit's expense. Further, it was validated that power can be useful in reducing low and moderate levels of conflict but will increase conflict when it is excessive. As with reward systems, one-sided interdependence or interdependence that allowed one unit to gain at another's expense, acted to cause conflict.

6

Personal-Behavior Factors

Personal-behavior factors specifically emphasize the human factors within the organization. We can differentiate them from structural factors in that, from the administrator's viewpoint, they are beyond his reach and must be accepted as generally uncontrollable by him. In this section we shall investigate the following variables to determine if they are conflict sources: personality, role satisfaction and status perception, personal goals, and informal social relationships.

PERSONALITY

An extensive review of the literature indicates that certain personality attributes increase conflict behavior.[1] Specifically, the empirical studies show the qualities of high authoritarianism, high dogmatism, and low self-esteem to be conflict sources.

Recent research findings on leadership style have generally downgraded autocracy. Emphasis has been redirected to selection of a style to

[1] R. E. Walton and R. B. McKersie, eds., *A Behavioral Theory of Labor Negotiations* (New York: McGraw-Hill Book Company, 1965).

reflect the leader, the led, and the situation.[2] Because no style is universally applicable and authoritarianism is frequently linked with the past, it appears intuitively correct that there would be a positive correlation between authoritarianism and conflict.

Again, intuitively we would expect a dogmatic personality to be a source of conflict because it would act to stifle change and innovation. Yet, it is difficult to reconcile this finding with our earlier conclusion that participation acts to increase conflict. One might speculate that if participation and conflict were positively correlated, a dogmatic personality should reduce conflict. The research to date does not support this speculation, and this relationship is clearly in need of further research.

The last personality factor cited, low self-esteem, implies that individuals who do not think highly of themselves would find others as threats and act to stimulate interpersonal antagonism. As with the two other personality characteristics, this too is intuitively logical.

ROLE SATISFACTION AND STATUS

Strong evidence is available to support the concept that organizational member's dissatisfaction with role requirements can be a source of conflict.

An analysis of purchasing agents' behavior demonstrated that when their status aspirations were blocked, the result was an increase in conflict with other units.[3] The same results were also generally found among individuals in staff positions.[4] Conclusions of studies on staff functioning indicate that if their status aspirations were frustrated, the staff perceived a lack of recognition for their efforts and inadequate opportunities for growth, which led these professionals to increasing conflict with other groups.

Both of the above studies are further supported by additional research.[5] In a study of officials' attitudes toward forms of conflict in the public domain, it was found that conflict was, to a great extent, a function of the role of the incumbent. Conflict could be explained in terms of the self-interests of the officials and the roles they occupied, which frequently overcame rationality.

The studies indicate that how one perceives himself in his position can significantly affect his performance and thus the potential for conflict between him and his peers in his own and adjoining units.

[2] Robert Tannenbaum and Warren H. Schmidt, "How to Choose a Leadership Pattern," *Harvard Business Review*, March/April, 1958, pp. 95-101.

[3] George Strauss, "Tactics of Lateral Relationship: The Purchasing Agent," *Administrative Science Quarterly*, September, 1962, pp. 161-86.

[4] Melville Dalton, *Men Who Manage* (New York: John Wiley and Sons, 1959).

[5] H. George Frederickson, "Role Occupancy and Attitudes Toward Labor Relations in Government," *Administrative Science Quarterly*, December, 1969, pp. 595-606.

The topic of status presents one of the truly interesting subjects in behavioral research. Members of organizations, almost unanimously will officially denounce their personal concern with the importance of status. Yet investigations into behavior validates status as a significant factor to every individual living in a civilized society. We are all quick to accuse others of being "status-seekers," but social scientists tell us that all advanced societies develop prestige gradings and individuals will seek to differentiate themselves from others through these gradings. When we recognize the importance of status, we should expect that conflict is stimulated where incongruencies occur in status gradings or from alterations in the status hierarchy. Our research supports this expectation.

An increase in conflict has been substantiated when the degree to which personal status, or how one perceives himself, and the level of departmental representation differed in rank ordering of status dimensions.[6] These dimensions included length of service, age, education, and pay. Similar results were obtained in another study.[7] It was observed that in an organization, where it was generally acknowledged that research had more prestige than engineering, patterns of initiation and influence were accepted when they followed this status ordering. But when this order was deviated from, as for example when low-status industrial engineers needed to direct the higher-status researchers in the implementing of tests, conflict resulted.

Whyte's [8] comprehensive investigation of the restaurant industry displayed similar conclusions. Conflict was found to result when low-status waitresses gave "orders" to high-status cooks. Due to the incongruity between initiation and status, cooks were being perceived in a lower prestige grade. These findings are closely paralleled by arguments presented by researchers,[9] who agree that conflict will result when one unit sets standards for another, where the former has the same or less status than the group for which it is setting standards.

GOALS

It has been postulated that conflict in organizations is inevitable.[10] The reasoning behind this view is that mutually exclusive structured interests are

[6] John M. Dutton and Richard E. Walton, "Interdepartmental Conflict and Cooperation: Two Contrasting Studies," *Human Organization,* Fall, 1966, pp. 207-21.

[7] J. A. Seiler, "Diagnosing Interdepartmental Conflict," *Harvard Business Review,* September/October, 1963, pp. 121-32.

[8] William F. Whyte, *Human Relations in the Restaurant Industry* (New York: McGraw-Hill Book Company, 1948).

[9] See Dalton, *op. cit.,* and Chris Argyris, *Integrating the Individual and the Organization* (New York: John Wiley and Sons, 1964).

[10] Ralf Dahrendorf, *Class and Class Conflict in Industrial Society* (London: Routledge and Kegan Paul, 1959).

universal in all societies and in all organizations, and therefore cannot be avoided. Specific evidence to support this claim has been similarly reached through investigation of departmentalized organizations.

As previously noted,[11] there is evidence to suggest that differing goals between production and sales and differing attitudes between line and staff units toward change as an objective are sources of conflict. Additionally, it has emphasized that conflict can arise from subgroups rationally pursuing different goals.[12]

The idea of conflicting goals has been further elaborated upon by others. One of specific interest postulates several differing goals that the researcher believes underlie many interdepartmental differences:[13] flexibility versus stability; short-run performance emphasis versus long-run; and maximizing organizational goals versus responding to other needs of the society.

SOCIAL INTERACTION

Two studies related social interaction to conflict, but they provided inconclusive evidence as to social interaction as a source of conflict.

The first study observed that there was a strong positive correlation between the rate of informal interaction and the ten conflict indices utilized in the study.[14] In contrast, another researcher found that frequency of social gatherings is positively correlated with conformity and negatively correlated, with conflict.[15] This latter finding cannot be reconciled with the first study, therefore making it difficult to generalize about social interaction as a source of conflict.

SUMMARY

This chapter surveyed personal-behavior variables as conflict sources. It was found that a high authoritarian, dogmatic, low self-esteem personality

[11] John M. Dutton and Richard E. Walton, "Interdepartmental Conflict and Cooperation: Two Contrasting Studies," *Human Organization,* Fall, 1966, pp. 207-21.

[12] Daniel Katz, "Approaches to Managing Conflict," in Robert L. Kahn and Elise Boulding's *Power and Conflict in Organizations* (New York: Basic Books, 1964), pp. 105-14.

[13] Henry A. Landsberger, "The Horizontal Dimension in Bureaucracy," *Administrative Science Quarterly,* December, 1961, pp. 299-332.

[14] Ronald G. Corwin, "Patterns of Organizational Conflict," *Administrative Science Quarterly,* December, 1969, pp. 507-20.

[15] Donald I. Warren, "The Effects of Power Bases and Peer Group on Conformity in Formal Organizations," *Administrative Science Quarterly,* December, 1969, pp. 544-56.

increased conflict. Dissatisfaction with role requirements in complex organizations was additionally supported as a source of conflict, as were incongruencies or alterations in the status hierarchy.

Where group goals are at odds, one would postulate that conflict would develop. Our research successfully supported this hypothesis. In contrast, opposed conclusions as to informal social interaction being a conflict source leaves us with inconclusive results on this variable.

III

ADMINISTRATIVE TOOLS

All skilled craftsmen require tools to perform their trade and the administrator is no exception. One cannot effectively manage without the appropriate tools.

Chapters 7 and 8 review the major tools for resolving conflict. The techniques suggested include problem solving, superordinate goals, avoidance, expansion of resources, smoothing, compromise, authoritative command, and changing of individuals and organization structures.

Chapter 9 develops tools for conflict stimulation. Though this area has been generally ignored by those concerned with conflict management, we have attempted to develop techniques relevant to the sources of conflict: communications, structure, and personal-behavior factors.

It is the objective of the following three chapters to present the reader with the resolution and stimulation tools necessary to be an effective conflict manager. The practicing administrator should become knowledgeable and proficient with each of the techniques presented.

7

Problem Solving

and Superordinate Goals

The major studies in the field of conflict have traditionally been obsessed with attempts to resolve the conflict state. While in Chapter 2 considerable emphasis was placed on the value of conflict, it nevertheless supported the view that resolution techniques were frequently required. In this chapter and the one that follows, these tools for reducing conflict will be presented.

Among the numerous methods of resolution that have been recognized, two have gained extremely strong support: problem solving and the use of superordinate goals. This support has developed from their success in reducing conflict through emphasis upon common interests between disagreeing parties. Our research indicates that where conditions are right for problem solving and/or superordinate goals, they should be given a high priority.

PROBLEM SOLVING

Blake, Shepard, and Mouton have proposed that mutual problem solving is the soundest method for resolving intergroup conflict.[1] The parties are

[1] Robert R. Blake, Herbert A. Shepard, and Jane S. Mouton, *Managing Intergroup Conflict in Industry* (Houston: Gulf Publishing Company, 1964), pp. 99-100.

required to come face-to-face with the underlying causes for their conflict, because it is they who share the responsibility for seeing that the solution works. These agreements seek to solve *the* problem rather than merely accommodate different points of view.

Mutual problem solving requires that the conflicting units have "the potential to achieve a better solution through collaboration." [2] Though this may be a difficult requirement to meet, where it exists, fundamental points of differences are sought rather than determination of who is right, who is wrong, who wins, or who loses. Further, through sharing and communicating, the problem is mutually defined. The participants, or at least their representatives, consider the full range of alternatives, and similarities in views become emphasized.[3] Through this process, the causes of doubt and misunderstanding that underlie the conflict become outwardly evident.

In contrast to other methods, which reinforce differences, problem solving additionally attempts to "accentuate-the-positive," by highlighting the commonly held views of the parties. This recognizes an often overlooked side of any conflict—that there exists in almost every instance some issues on which the dissenting parties are in agreement. These similarities are too frequently by-passed, and results in what has been referred to by Coleman [4] as Gresham's Law of Conflict. Coleman states that similar views and those that work to increase cooperation are pushed out by those views that accentuate differences. Bad forces push out the good. Problem solving seeks to emphasize the similar views and avoid those that breed a hostile climate.

The attempt to resolve differences through the problem-solving approach as described above is frequently used, and unfortunately, evidence indicates it frequently fails. How often we hear someone who is aware of the existence of a conflict say, "What they need to do is sit down and discuss the situation." But problem solving is limited in the types of conflict it can deal with effectively. Its failures are closely related to its misapplication. Clearly, it is most successful in semantic conflicts. Oppositions that develop from misunderstandings lend themselves to the in-depth analysis of problem solving, definition of terms, and thorough understanding of the opposing parties' ideas.

Even in those instances where conditions appear right for successful problem solving, the process of reduction may be a lengthy one if the conflict has existed for some time. Blake, Shepard, and Mouton found in their experiments with the use of problem solving in union-management relation-

[2] *Ibid.,* p. 86.

[3] *Ibid.,* pp. 90-93.

[4] James S. Coleman, *Community Conflict* (New York: Free Press of Glencoe, 1957), p. 14.

ships that great patience was needed to reduce long-standing existent conflict.

> Correcting a situation of long term chronic hostility requires continuous and diligent followup efforts. As much as a five-year span may be needed before the root system that produced the original animosities can be replaced by a new and healthier root system—one that can cause a relationship to flourish.[5]

As will become apparent in Chapter 10, problem solving is inherently weak in regard to conflicts based on differing value systems—one of the primary sources of conflict. A dispute over the merits of racial integration between two individuals with conflicting value systems demonstrates this point. It would be naive to assume that Mr. Jones, raised to believe blacks and whites are unquestionably equal, and Mr. Smith, raised in an environment that fostered a belief in the inequality of blacks and whites, can resolve their differences through problem solving. Such an approach can get to the root of the conflict, which unfortunately in this case, is two *incompatible* value systems. This attempt to reduce differences through problem solving will undoubtedly result in Mr. Jones' recognition that Mr. Smith is a "prejudiced bigot," and Mr. Smith's belief that Mr. Jones is "an ignorant liberal who doesn't realize that there are tangible and meaningful differences in the races, and that the Good Lord meant that they be separated." Such forced problem solving only widens the differences and entrenches each of the participants deeper into his position—for all intents and purposes probably increasing, and certainly not lessening, the level of conflict.

SUPERORDINATE GOALS

Superordinate goals are complementary to, and frequently a natural evolvement from problem solving. A survey of the applied conflict management literature finds rather enthusiastic support for this method in reducing social conflict and increasing the likelihood of achieving stated objectives.[6]

---

[5] Robert R. Blake, Herbert A. Shepard and Jane S. Mouton, *Managing Intergroup Conflict in Industry* (Houston: Gulf Publishing Company, 1964), p. 194.

[6] See Muzafer Sherif, *In Common Predicament: Social Psychology of Intergroup Conflict and Cooperation* (Boston: Houghton Mifflin Company, 1966), *Intergroup Relations and Leadership* (New York: John Wiley and Sons, 1962); Muzafer Sherif and Carolyn W. Sherif, *Groups in Harmony and Tension* (New York: Harper and Brothers, 1953); Daniel Katz and Robert L. Kahn, *The Social Psychology of Organizations* (New York: John Wiley and Sons, 1966); Herbert L. Thelen, *Dynamics of Groups at Work* (Chicago: University of Chicago Press, 1954).

The superordinate goal is similar to a common goal because it requires mutual dependence between two or more groups. But, the superordinate goal is more because it is "compelling and highly appealing . . . which cannot be attained by the resources of any single group separately." [7] It is based on interdependency.

A superordinate goal initiates with a definition of a shared goal and the recognition that without the help of the contending parties, it cannot be attained. While each unit desires them, they are unattainable to any single unit. Superordinate goals are highly valued, unattainable by any one group alone, and commonly sought. They must, to be effective, supersede other goals that the units may individually have. They act to reduce conflict by requiring the disagreeing parties to work together in achieving those goals they mutually seek.

After extensive research of resolution techniques, Sherif concluded that in those instances where conflict has developed from mutually incompatible goals, the use of superordinate goals, based on mutual interdependence, should increase cooperation.[8] The cooperative environment grows as effort is directed away from concern with separate and independent units to recognition that the conflicting units are part of a larger group; a synergy developing from the collaboration of forces.

In the early 1970s, General Motors used a superordinate goal in their effort to unite labor and management against the threat of imported automobiles. A new, highly automated production assembly facility was built in Lordstown, Ohio to produce the Chevrolet Vega, GM's answer to the foreign subcompact. The corporation sought high quality and high volume output, but desired to reduce anticipated labor-management tensions in the most modern auto plant in the United States. Management decided to implement a campaign intended to unify the workers in an effort to counter the threat posed to the American auto market by the rapidly increasing number of cars being imported. They viewed this cause to be one which would be highly valued, unattainable by any one group alone, and commonly sought.

> To instill workers with a sense of mission, signs festooned the plant reminding that they were the front line of defense against foreign imports. 'Product excellence makes our jobs secure,' trumpeted one sign.[9]

[7] Muzafer Sherif, "Experiments on Group Conflict and Cooperation," in Leavitt and Pondy's *Readings in Managerial Psychology* (Chicago: University of Chicago Press, 1964), p. 410.

[8] Muzafer Sherif, *In Common Predicament: Social Psychology of Intergroup Conflict and Cooperation* (Boston: Houghton Mifflin Company, 1966), p. 93.

[9] Jon Lowell, "GMAD: Lowdown at Lordstown," *Ward's Auto World,* April, 1972, p. 29.

General Motors' effort to resolve conflicts through rallying both workers and management around the superordinate goal of survival has to be described as a failure, given the open violence and strike that took place in 1972. One major reason may have been the inadequacy of the goal itself. Apparently, few employees were credulous enough to believe the increased sale of imports in the United States as a threat to the largest industrial firm in the world.

VALUE AND LIMITATIONS

The popularity of the use of superordinate goals is undoubtedly a result of their emphasis on cooperation and the potential for each party to win, or at the worst, not lose. Thelen,[10] an active supporter of superordinate goals, views them as a simple solution for resolving conflict, for all that is required is that members of the two groups work together on some project in which their representativeness to their own group is irrelevant, but in which the efforts of members of both groups are required for success. This simplicity though is frequently lost in practice where we find applicable superordinate goals considerably more difficult to develop than theoretical ones.

Sherif believes that there is wide potential for the use of these goals except where "the goal of one group is annihilation or exploitation of the other." [11] But other limitations are too restrictive for wider acceptance. First, it is frequently difficult to create situations where individuals will work together and ignore the differences between them. A common goal, which requires the involvement of all parties and which additionally will supersede individual group goals, is often difficult to create. Thelen refers to bringing groups *A* and *B* together to form a new group *C,* but notes that the "goals must be defined in such a way that there is no jurisdictional overlap with *A* and *B*." [12] Theoretically this does not sound as difficult as is the task of developing and implementing such superordinate goals. Secondly, a characteristic that is missing in many conflicts is that the disagreeing parties have mutual trust and confidence in each other and that individual member objectives are not thwarted.

> Superordinate goals are possible only when two or more groups find a purpose toward which each can strive without sacrificing the most cher-

[10] Herbert L. Thelen, *Dynamics of Groups at Work* (Chicago: University of Chicago Press, 1954), p. 350.

[11] Muzafer Sherif, *In Common Predicament: Social Psychology of Intergroup Conflict and Cooperation* (Boston: Houghton Mifflin Company, 1966), p. 107.

[12] Herbert L. Thelen, *Dynamics of Groups at Work* (Chicago: University of Chicago Press, 1954), pp. 350-51.

ished aspirations of its members. When this is not possible, group conflict continues despite efforts to forestall its ultimate consequences and despite practices that appear legitimate to each group.[13]

Finally, while the superordinate goal instituted in a problem-solving environment may have outstanding results where the source of conflict is semantic in nature, its potential is severely limited where the conflict germinates from personal-behavior differences. As was presented earlier in this chapter, in those areas where value clashes are the cause of conflict, attempts to define the problem and seek the source of the differences only entrenches the conflicting views and widens the gap that already exists. Thus, when used with problem solving, superordinate goals have the same limitations as problem solving.

AN EMPIRICAL INVESTIGATION

One of the most comprehensive and illuminating experiments in developing a conflict environment and utilizing superordinate goals to achieve resolution has been reported by Sherif.[14]

The participants in his study were healthy and normal eleven and twelve-year old boys in a summer camp environment. The research progressed through three stages: (1) development of two separate groups of boys, (2) formation of hostility between the two groups, and (3) the attempt to resolve the conflict that had developed in stage two.

Each group was taken to the camp separately and allowed to get established, neither being aware of the other's existence. While they were at the same location, the size of the camp made physical separation possible. The separate groups established themselves, and developed group norms of behavior as the researchers had hypothesized they would. They partook in camping activities and enjoyed opportunities for healthy competition among themselves. This completed stage one and prepared the campers for stage two.

Stage two was accomplished by making each group aware of the other and by emphasizing that certain activities that were enjoyed by both were scarce. Win-lose situations were established so that what was available for group *A* was unavailable to group *B* and vice-versa. As a result, bitter resentment, overtly demonstrated in talk and action, developed between the

[13] Muzafer Sherif, *In Common Predicament: Social Psychology of Intergroup Conflict and Cooperation* (Boston: Houghton Mifflin Company, 1966), p. 107.

[14] Adapted from Muzafer Sherif, *In Common Predicament: Social Psychology of Intergroup Conflict and Cooperation.* Houghton Mifflin Co., 1966. Used by permission.

two groups. The resentment produced major changes in attitudes toward the out-group. Additionally, changes occurred within the group. Stronger ties were developed internally, as were changes in leadership to align with the new goals. Interestingly, experiments to test changes in judgment of members and out-group performance found that members perceived those individuals in their own group as making better judgments and performing skills with greater precision than those in the other group, although in actuality there were no differences. Attitudes were adopted within each group so as to facilitate extreme criticism of all members of the other group. Membership in the other unit became the only requirement for individuals of one group to openly despise the other. Conflict increased and reached a zenith in open warfare. The campers had supported two of Sherif's hypotheses in this stage: (1) when members of two groups come into contact with one another in a series of activities that embody goals which each actively seeks, but which can only be attained by one at the expense of the other, competitive activity will change into hostility between the groups and their members, and (2) the conflict *between* the groups will tend to stimulate an increase in solidarity *within* each group. Sherif and his associates then prepared for the third and final stage of the study—that of attempting to resolve the conflict.

Sherif considered several conflict resolution methods. Accurate and favorable information dispensed about the opposing group was not seen in a favorable light nor was a conference of leaders. Appeals to the moral values of brotherly love, cooperation, and forgiveness of the enemies' deeds were made in sermons during religious services at camp, but they had no effect. The introduction of a common enemy had only a temporary impact. By using superordinate goals, it was postulated that conflict could be reduced and finally eliminated. Those goals utilized included a "planned" breakdown of the water supply, the cooperative selection of a motion picture, and the "planned" breakdown of the camp truck that was needed to obtain food. The researchers purposely broke the water line and then informed the separate groups of the crisis. Both promptly volunteered to search the water line for the trouble. But once the break was found, the previous hostile behavior between the groups returned. When both groups wanted a movie, they were told that the camp could not afford two separate films. The groups got together, chose a film by a common vote, and viewed it as one group. When the researchers arranged for the breakdown of the camp truck, which was scheduled to go to town for groceries, it became necessary for both groups to pitch-in and push the vehicle to get it started.

The above-mentioned cumulative superordinate goals gradually reduced conflict and hostility between the groups. There was no immediate reduction of hostility, but the reinforcement of dependence helped to alleviate separatism and opposition. Sherif concluded that these reinforced superordinate goals developed procedures for cooperating in specific activities which had transfer value for new situations, thereby establishing modes of intergroup cooperation. As the study came to its end, interactions between members of the previously opposing groups were overtly friendly. When the alternatives of separate buses or a single bus were discussed for the trip home, the latter was sought by the majority. The one group that had five dollars left from a prize won in competition used it to buy refreshments on the trip home—not for just its members, but for the campers in both groups. Evidently the hostility created in stage two had been eminently reduced.

Sherif [15] concluded some important points from the study, applicable to any conflict situation. First, all the boys had been carefully selected for normality, health, and social adjustment. Given these quite normal subjects, hostility could be created and thus can be said to be characteristic of certain conditions—i.e., two groups competing for goals that only one group could attain—and not a result of neurotic tendencies of individuals. Second, co-operative and democratic procedures within groups were not directly transferable to intergroup relations. On the contrary, cooperativeness and solidarity within groups were at their height when intergroup conflict was most severe. Third, conflict was not reduced by contact between group representatives, even though contiguous and pleasant conditions were created. Fourth, contact between groups involving interdependent actions towards superordinate goals was conducive to intergroup cooperation, but single episodes of cooperation were not sufficient to reduce established intergroup hostility and negative stereotypes. And lastly, a series of cooperative situations toward superordinate goals had cumulative effect in reducing intergroup hostility. This cumulative effect involves the successful development of procedures and their transfer to new situations, so that established roles of intergroup cooperation are recognized.

The experiment demonstrated the value of common goals in resolving conflicts. Of course, one must admit the possibility that children react differently than adults to conflict stimulation and resolution. But due to the overriding value of superordinate goals in those situations conducive to their use, the administrator should consider them highly effective tools for resolving conflict levels. In the next chapter, other popular methods for conflict resolution will be presented and discussed.

[15] Muzafer Sherif, "Experiments on Group Conflict and Cooperation," in Leavitt and Pondy's *Readings in Managerial Psychology* (Chicago: University of Chicago Press, 1954), pp. 408-21.

8

Other
Resolution
Techniques

The previous chapter presented the most frequently employed methods of conflict resolution—problem solving and the use of superordinate goals. In this section seven additional techniques to reduce or eliminate conflict will be presented: (1) expansion of resources, (2) avoidance, (3) smoothing, (4) compromise, (5) authoritative command, (6) altering the human variable, and (7) altering the structural variable. Each of the techniques developed on the following pages has proven successful in reducing or eliminating various types of dysfunctional conflict. Each method is presented, not to be viewed as a self-contained solution, but as one of many tools in the manager's tool box. In some instances, one "tool" alone may be sufficient, while at other times several may be needed simultaneously.

EXPANSION OF RESOURCES

When conflict is predicated upon the scarcity of a resource, the easiest manner in which to resolve the confrontation, and the one most satisfying to the conflicting parties, is through expansion of the available resources. Although it may be most undesirable to other parties outside the conflict, its greatest strength as a resolution tool is in its ability to allow each conflicting party a victory.

If the purchasing department in a moderate-sized school district is allocated only $1,500 for salary increases, to be distributed among the department's four members, any individual's gain is at the expense of others in the unit. Our example in Chapter 3 of Professors Jones and Smith, who were each striving for the single promotion to be given for the coming year, created a situation where one gains at another's expense. Both the conflicts represent a zero-sum game, having developed from a fixed resource quantity where demand for a resource exceeds its supply. More money for salary increases in the purchasing department or more promotion opportunities in Professor Smith and Jones's department at the university could effectively resolve the above conflicts.

This technique was effectively used in 1969, when the presidency of the Ford Motor Company was left vacant by the departure of Semon Knudsen. Three vice-presidents were prime candidates for the position. The decision of who would be promoted to the presidency rested with the company's chairman, Henry Ford II, but a decision to give one of the aspirants the position would have resulted in only one winner and two losers. Hence, the three vice-presidents' desire for a limited resource, the company's presidency, created a conflict. Henry Ford's decision to create an Office of the President resolved the conflict through expansion. The position was expanded, enabling each of the three aspirants to become president over a specific jurisdiction. By increasing the scarce resource, supply was expanded to meet the demand. This solution resolved the conflict by directly altering its source and thus creating three winners.

Expanding resources as a resolution method is extremely successful because it leaves the conflicting parties satisfied. But its use is restricted by the nature of its inherent limitation that resources rarely exist in such quantity as to be easily expanded. Although not commonly referred to in the conflict resolution literature, the method is presented here to emphasize its ability to reduce hostility and to offer an easy alternative to the administrator, if and when it is applicable. As will be discussed in Chapter 10, its application is restricted to resolving conflicts that arise from structural sources.

AVOIDANCE

The most natural manner in which all animals, including man, eliminate conflict is to avoid it. When we withdraw from the arena of confrontation, we effectively avoid conflict. While it has not been resolved in any permanent way, it can be a successful short-run alternative.

Avoidance through withdrawal is a behavior seen frequently among administrators. Chester Barnard observed nearly four decades ago that men generally try to avoid decisions.[1] Barnard categorized decisions into two major classes, ". . . positive decisions—to do something, to direct action, to cease action, to prevent action; and negative decisions, which are decisions not to decide." [2] Awareness that any positive decision can cause conflict frequently results in the administrator withdrawing from the arena by deciding not to decide. Withdrawal describes a frequently exhibited behavior when differences develop between individuals or groups within an organization. To evade overt demonstration of disagreement, each party acknowledges physical separation and stakes out a territory that is distinct from the other. The employee who finds that he and his boss have difficulty agreeing on most any subject can seek this technique as a solution. In those cases where the employee sees no other viable alternative to his present job and his superior finds the employee's performance to be satisfactory, we can expect this avoidance technique to be effective.

In addition to withdrawal, suppression is another form of avoidance. Like withdrawal, suppression does not resolve into a defeat or victory situation. No side wins, but no side loses either. In contrast to our withdrawing example above, the superior and subordinate may find that evading each other is not possible or desirous. In that case, the conflict may be resolvable by each withholding his or her feelings or beliefs. Clearly, it is a less-than-optimum resolution method because it really only conceals differences. Yet Shepard has described this avoidance technique as "society's chief instrument for handling conflict." [3] Although many, if not most, interpersonal conflicts exist latently, they are nonetheless conflicts and can be resolved by the individual parties' avoidance of overt confrontation.

SMOOTHING

Smoothing, as described by Blake and Mouton,[4] is the process of playing down differences that exist between individuals or groups while emphasizing common interests. Those issues upon which differences exist are not openly

[1] Chester I. Barnard, *The Functions of the Executive* (Cambridge: Harvard University Press, 1938), p. 189.

[2] *Ibid.,* p. 194.

[3] "Responses to Situations of Competition and Conflict," by Herbert Shepard, in *Power and Conflict in Organizations,* edited by Robert L. Kahn and Elise Boulding, © 1964 by the Foundation for Research on Human Behavior, Basic Books, Inc., Publishers, New York.

[4] Robert R. Blake and Jane S. Mouton, *Managerial Grid* (Houston: Gulf Publishing Company, 1964).

discussed. Communication revolves around similarly held views, which are held by the opposing parties.

In our discussion of suppression, it was noted that differences were withheld or concealed. In smoothing, we continue to suppress differences but additionally accentuate similarities. When applied to conflict the use of this technique can act as a countervailing force to Gresham's Law. By returning to our previously described boss/subordinate conflict, smoothing could be applied to this interaction. In addition to utilizing withdrawing or suppression techniques, their relationship could be improved by each attempting to find points on which similar views are shared. Smoothing, therefore, is not totally unlike that of reinforced superordinate goals. The end result is the realization by each conflicting unit that the other's position is not necessarily as polarized as was generally believed. By working together toward a common goal or emphasizing common interests, both superordinate goals and smoothing accentuate similarities and deemphasize differences.

Although smoothing is a technique often used for handling organizational conflict, it is only a superficial resolution. The differences, which are not explicitly confronted, still remain, and it becomes only a matter of time before these dissimilarities arise again. Therefore, like avoidance, its strength lies in the short term and in those situations where a temporary solution is sought.

COMPROMISE

Compromise techniques make up the major portion of resolution methods developed in the literature. Included in this classification are external or third-party intervention, plus internal compromise between conflicting parties through both total group and representative negotiation and voting.

A compromised decision, like avoidance, does not result in either a distinct loser or a decisive winner. Unlike avoidance, it does result in a decision, though not an optimum one for either party. A compromise resolution is executed by rationing the object of the conflict or, where not divisible, one can reward the other by yielding something of substitute value. Its distinguishing characteristic is that it requires each party to give up something.

Negotiations between unions and management over wages, hours, and working conditions are a classic example of conflict bargaining where compromise is utilized as a resolution technique. Traditionally, labor's representatives come to the negotiation with a list of demands. In anticipation that they will have to reduce these demands, the union asks for far more than they believe realistically attainable. In contrast, management seeks to meet as few of the demands as they deem possible. Compromising follows the initial demand and counter offer; the union presents an extensive list of demands and management counters with usually little more than the terms of the current, soon to expire, contract. The negotiators then seek to find a balance acceptable to the groups they represent. When each group is negotiating from strength and is knowledgeable about the adversary, the final accord that is reached represents a compromise; that is, each party will have had to give up something of value. In those instances where either management or union strength is undeniably superior to the other, the negotiation may involve little compromising, resulting in a win/lose situation. Therefore, the relative strength of the bargaining parties will determine the extent of compromising that will take place.

Though compromising is a universal and frequently used method of resolving conflict between individuals or groups, when representatives are established to resolve an intergroup conflict, such as in our union-management example, the resolving negotiations are less effective. The problem develops from the representative's position as negotiating leader. He has been placed in a leadership position because he holds the trust of the group and will be expected to represent the views held by his constituencies. But in the bargaining process, any signs shown by this leader of his willingness to compromise demonstrates weakness in the constituency's view and threatens his power position. Should he be in a position to resolve the issue so as to make his group a clear winner, at the expense of the other, he returns a hero. Should the compromise be made at his group's expense, the leader returns a loser and finds his leadership position deteriorated. Therefore, "giving in" on some of the demands of the adversary may significantly alter his leadership effectiveness with his group, but it is this compromising that is necessary to achieve resolution.

Third-party interventions through arbitration or judicial settlement are methods of compromise, but they successfully avoid the potential "traitor" characteristics that exist in the representative role. These two methods free the group leader from peer pressure by relegating the burden of the final decision to an impartial third party. Now the third party becomes the focal point. If labor and management negotiations reach a stalemate, compromise may be achieved by a third party arbitrating a settlement.

Should the decision handed down by the third party be favorable to one group, the arbitrator is seen as "perceptive and wise" by the winner. In contrast, the losers will view the judge as "a weak thinker," "blind to facts," or "biased." Third-party judgment is a compromise, yet in those instances where one or both parties believe it has been misjudged, it allows hostility to be directed to the arbiter and away from the conflicting parties. Intervention by a third party appears to be most effective where the arbitrator has succeeded in convincing each conflicting unit that it has won a victory.

The final area of compromise we shall consider is voting. Here democratic procedures allow disagreeing parties to resolve their differences on a majority-wins basis. Although democratic in nature, it infrequently appeases the minority faction as it allows the most powerful group to exert its strength by overpowering the weaker group. But voting, as do all techniques that utilize compromise, does not get to the cause of the conflict. Compromise techniques succeed only in manipulating the end results and fail in altering the conditions leading to those ends. Hence conflict is only temporarily reduced or eliminated. The temporality of compromise may explain why it is the most frequently used of resolution techniques. Because it is short lived, it is necessary that it be initiated often.

AUTHORITATIVE COMMAND

In formal organizational structures, where superior-subordinate relationships exist, the authority of a higher-ranking individual is the most frequent resolvent of interpersonal or intergroup conflict. Although formal authority is also a form of arbitration, it has been separated here to denote its wide acceptance in complex organizations as a resolution tool.

A disagreement between two nurses that cannot be resolved between them is taken to their immediate supervisor or head nurse for a decision. In this same manner, when a conflict develops between sales and production units within a manufacturing organization, it is referred to the two immediate executives responsible for each function and who possess the authority to resolve the differences. If an agreement cannot be reached at this level, the authority of their mutual superior will act as the ultimate judge and, in the majority of cases, will be accepted by both parties.

Individuals in organizations, with rare exceptions, recognize and accept the authority of their superiors. Though they may not be in agreement with these decisions, they will almost always abide by them. Thus, authoritative command is highly successful in achieving reduced conflict levels. But, like compromise techniques, a superior's authority only eliminates the resulting conflict and not the seed from which it generates.

ALTERING THE HUMAN VARIABLE

Where conflicts are significant and when their dysfunctionality becomes a severe cost to the organization, alteration of one or more of the conflicting parties' behavior may be necessary. While such techniques are slow and frequently quite costly, the results can be substantial. Furthermore, in contrast to smoothing, compromise, or formal authority, changing the behavior of the human variable has the potential to alleviate the source of conflict as well as the end conflict itself. In other words, while it will take longer to achieve, it frequently results in long term and more meaningful harmony.

Traditionally, the vehicle for behavioral change has been education. This has been primarily in the area of human relations training, but has also included educating the organization members to reinforce loyalty to the organization's rules and ideology when the conflict is based on individual-organizational differences. There is some evidence to support reading and discussion as a means for individuals to alter their values and attitudes towards others and to the superordinate organization.

Of more recent vintage has been the development of laboratory training, which seeks to change values and attitudes through a group process. Also referred to as T-group or sensitivity training, it influences the participants through unstructured group interaction. Members are brought together in a free and open environment, loosely directed by a professional behavioral scientist. This professional then creates the opportunity for participants to express their ideas, beliefs, and attitudes. Successful laboratory training will increase an individual's awareness of how he is perceived by others, and thereby expand his knowledge of himself. Additionally, it improves the participant's listening ability and understanding of others. This latter result gives each member insight into how others feel about various subjects and improves the participant's ability to empathize. When it effectively breaks through the role facades that each member has built around himself, laboratory training has had success in reducing interpersonal and intergroup conflicts.

ALTERING STRUCTURAL VARIABLES

The last major category of resolution techniques seeks to reduce conflict by altering the formal organization structure. Major options available within this technique are transferring and exchanging group members, creating coordinating positions, developing an appeals system, and expanding the group's or organization's boundaries.

When we encounter intraorganizational conflict, early consideration should be given to transferring the conflicting member or members out of the unit. By removing this negative force, we may be able to easily, quickly, and effectively reduce the tensions that exist. Organizations will also occasionally alter departments or other structural units so as to cross-fertilize those areas in conflict and force contact between members. This can be done by actually transferring individuals between units or by creating a co-ordinator to act as a buffer between the units.

When we exchange members between organizational units, we bring to each group a new perspective. Previous organizational barriers are often reduced. A manager at a production plant for one of the major U.S. aluminum companies employed the idea of employee exchange to reduce conflict in his accounting department. The plant controller attributed the dysfunctional behavior between his general accounting and cost accounting sections to the lack of an information flow between each group. The two units were frequently at odds with each other. To reduce misunderstandings, he had the supervisors of both sections switch jobs for a six month period. In addition to increasing departmental flexibility, the move successfully expanded the perspective of each supervisor, which promoted greater understanding and reduced intergroup conflict as the modified views filtered down through each's section.

Creating new buffer positions can stimulate the same effect. On occasion, when industrial firms have conflicts, such as between accounting and engineering departments, they will seek an individual with both an accounting and engineering background, and then create the position of coordinator for him. He functions then as an integrator between the separate units.

The Ombudsman fills this integrating-buffer position today at many larger colleges and universities. The rapid enrollment growth in higher education during the 1960s placed heavy pressures on the collegial organization. As we would expect, given the discussion in Chapter 5, with an increase in an institution's size, the number and intensity of conflicts increases. Problems were arising at all levels: among and between faculty, students, and staff. The Ombudsman position was created to mediate these differences, especially the ever increasing disputes between students and faculty and between faculty and the administration.

William Scott [5] advocates altering the structure when he suggests a formalized appeal system through which members of a bureaucratic organization can appeal if they believe their rights have been jeopardized. This altered structure allows members the right of formal redress. This opportunity to challenge a superior's action then acts as a restraint on arbitrary and unjustified use of formal authority. By giving the subordinate an alternative to unsatisfactory directives of his superior, it can act to reduce conflict by requiring the superior to rethink the legitimacy of the demands he makes upon his subordinates.

[5] William G. Scott, *The Management of Conflict* (Homewood, Illinois: Richard D. Irwin, 1965).

The college Ombudsman was described as maintaining a buffer position, but as one might expect, the position can also function in a judicial capacity within an appeals system. The Ombudsman may hold authority to hear and act upon perceived injustices within the college community.

Unionized organizations present an excellent illustration of the appeals technique. In their grievance procedure, unions have established an elaborate appeals system to resolve conflicts with management. If an aggrieved union member cannot find satisfaction through discussion with his superior, he may proceed to appeal his grievance upward through his employing organization; a frequent route in an industrial setting may include presenting his case to the area foreman, shift foreman, plant superintendent, industrial relations manager, plant manager, and eventually presenting his case to a neutral arbitrator, if necessary.

Another method of structural change is frequently presented in organizational theory. When an organization finds itself confronting conflict, it will seek to expand its boundaries and include the conflicting units.[6] This expansion technique is exemplified by the solution applied to the conflicts generated when a College of Business' curriculum must rely heavily upon the economics courses offered in the Economics department. Historically, economics was located in the College of Arts and Sciences or Liberal Arts. The philosophical conflicts that often develop between the two can be reconciled through expansion of the business program to include the Economics department. The result is the frequently encountered "College of Business and Economics." Elementary and secondary school systems utilize this same technique when they allow persons critical of the curriculum to participate in the review and evaluation of the system's programs and policies.

COMPARING PREFERENCES FOR RESOLUTION TECHNIQUES

Ronald Burke of York University [7] undertook a study to determine the effectiveness and ineffectiveness of various types of resolution techniques. He asked fifty-seven subjects to think of a time when they felt especially good or bad about the way an interpersonal conflict was resolved, and then to

[6] See Daniel Katz and Robert L. Kahn, *The Social Psychology of Organizations* (New York: John Wiley and Sons, Inc., 1966); James D. Thompson, *Organizations in Action* (New York: McGraw-Hill Book Company, 1967); and Philip Selznick, *TVA and the Grass Roots* (Berkeley, California: University of California Press, 1953).

[7] Ronald J. Burke, "Methods of Resolving Interpersonal Conflict," *Personnel Administration*, July, 1969, pp. 48-55.

describe it in detail. Burke then coded their responses into one of five methods suggested by Blake, Shepard, and Mouton: [8] withdrawing, smoothing, compromising, forcing, and problem solving. His findings, in Table 8–1,

TABLE 8–1

METHODS ASSOCIATED WITH EFFECTIVE AND
INEFFECTIVE CONFLICT RESOLUTION

	Effective Resolution %	Ineffective Resolution %
Withdrawal *	0.0	9.4
Smoothing	0.0	1.9
Compromise	11.3	5.7
Forcing *	24.5	79.2
Problem Solving *	58.5	0.0
Other (still unresolved; unable to determine how resolved, etc.)	5.7	3.8

* Percentage difference between groups is significant at the .05 level of confidence.

Source: Adapted from Ronald J. Burke, "Methods of Resolving Superior-Subordinate Conflict: The Constructive Use of Subordinate Differences and Disagreements," *Organizational Behavior and Human Performance,* July, 1970, p. 403.

represent percentage responses derived from the descriptions of effective and ineffective resolutions offered by the subjects. Though Blake and Mouton's categories do not fit precisely with those presented in this and the previous chapter and are limited in their comprehensiveness, Burke's findings are meaningful and his terms can be reconciled with this presentation.

Where resolutions of conflict were perceived to be effective, problem solving was the most common method (58.5%), followed by forcing (24.5%), and compromise (11.3%). Forcing, in Blake and Mouton's definition, refers to a win-lose situation and closely parallels this writer's category of authoritative command. When resolution methods were perceived as ineffective, forcing was the most commonly referenced method (79.2%), followed by withdrawal with only 9.4%.

Burke concluded from this study that force was perceived as an effective method of resolving conflict by the victor, but not by the vanquished. When forcing was effective, it was perceived as such by the winner, and when ineffective it was perceived in this manner by the loser. Additionally, problem solving was found to be significantly superior in reducing conflict.

[8] Robert R. Blake, Herbert Shepard, and Jane Mouton, *Managing Intergroup Conflict in Industry* (Houston: Gulf Publishing Company, 1964).

Though Burke's study was limited in size, it gives strong support to problem solving. However, there is a significant limitation to the value of these findings. They do not refer to the attainment of organization objectives but only upon the perceptions of individuals. We suggest that there may be a great differential between methods that alleviate conflict and satisfy individuals and those that alleviate conflict and satisfy organizational goals. From the administrative perspective established in Chapter 1, we should be concerned with the latter.

SUMMARY

In this chapter seven major areas of conflict resolution techniques were presented. Each has its own strengths and weaknesses. The material presented in these past two chapters has prepared the administrator to meet conflict situations with the right tools, but they require considerable understanding and practice to be utilized effectively.

In closing this chapter, a pessimistic note should be made. Occasionally, the administrator has to accept the reality that he will be required to cope with situations where he is powerless to resolve the conflict. In those situations where he cannot influence the situation, we suggest that it is best that he not frustrate himself in trying to control that which cannot be controlled. Hopefully, these uncontrollable occasions will be infrequent.

9

Stimulation

Techniques

In Chapter 2 conflict management was defined as the planning and evaluating of conflict levels. This is a broader interpretation than the historical definition of conflict management as the study of conflict resolution. In Chapters 7 and 8 the more traditional methods of conflict resolution techniques were presented. In this chapter, however, another dimension of conflict management is developed. In this section the reader will be presented with what may previously have been an unheard of objective: development of techniques for increasing interpersonal and intergroup conflict.

It is not easy for the administrator to change his managerial style and attitudes toward conflict overnight. But before change can take place, there must be new information made available and it is in this chapter that this information is presented. It can be expected that the administrator will find his role as "peacemaker" and "wound healer" more secure than his role as conflict stimulator, if only because it is the more familiar. However, the administrator's responsibility to the organization overrides his personal uneasiness, an uneasiness that will only be temporary. The manager who understands and has experienced both roles of conflict resolver and conflict stimulator is prepared to optimize his unit's performance and reap the satisfaction that comes from creating a dynamic, aggressive, creative, and successful unit.

The manager is being asked to develop a new perspective; one that accepts conflict, and further seeks to manipulate it in the best interest of achieving his organization's goals. Gone is the belief that a good manager is one who fosters tranquility. In his new role the manager recognizes that with peace comes apathy. And if apathy exists today, can deterioration be far behind?

The following pages seek to offer some ideas for increasing conflict between individuals and between groups. No claim can be made that the methods presented here comprehensively cover available stimulation techniques. In actuality, they are the expansion of those sources found to create conflict, which were presented in Chapter 4 through Chapter 6. These suggestions are only a beginning upon which both researchers and practitioners can expand.

The approach taken here is developed from the model presented in Chapter 3; conflict $= f$(communication, structure, and personal-behavior factors). Any change among these variables will alter conflict levels. Consequently, conflict stimulation, as did resolution, must develop from those methods that will increase organizational conflict by altering one or more of the three variables.

COMMUNICATION

As demonstrated in Chapter 3, communication is achieved through both words and actions. Through these words and actions, administrators can strongly influence levels of conflict. This is particularly true at the top administrative levels within an organization. The attitude at the top has dramatic impact on the behavior of all other organizational members.

It has also been previously noted that conflict will occur within any organization, and that the top administrative group cannot completely eliminate it, even if that were its goal. In those environments where conflict is communicated, through words and/or actions, as being evil, and therefore openly disapproved of, we can expect it to withdraw underground. But such conflict will frequently be dysfunctional to the attainment of organization objectives. Only by acknowledging conflict and developing an environment where conflict is encouraged, can the administrator control it. A positive communique concerning conflict allows the manager to establish levels of desired conflict, compare actual against this desired standard, and to take action, if necessary, to correct deviations.

This acknowledgment of "top-down" communication is a recognition that the organizational environment, created by top management, can stimulate conflict through supportive communication. Therefore, managed conflict stimulation requires the top administration to communicate down throughout the organization its philosophy that functional conflict is encouraged. This is transmitted through both words and actions. Each is necessary to develop a consistent and supportive environment for conflict. Words that are contradicted by actions will clearly be ineffective in creating this environment. Only through reconcilable verbal and nonverbal communication can the top administration create the appropriate setting.

Once those in the organization perceive that functional conflict is supported by top management, it is possible for managers to openly strive to manage it. Since we have demonstrated methods of conflict resolution, we now can present methods for its stimulation through communication. However, it must be remembered that none of these methods will be openly utilized unless our first communication requirement, encouragement by top management, exists.

A primary method for increasing conflict is manipulating the communication channels. This includes deviating messages from traditional channels, repression of information, transmission of too much information about other individuals or units, and communication of ambiguous or threatening information.

Deviations from Traditional Channels

Two basic ways exist for the administrator to deviate communication from the standard channels: formally and informally. The former is a purposeful alteration of the channels by which communications pass within the formal organizational structure. Individuals or groups who previously were included in the information patterns as a result of their position and status in the organization can be by-passed. Further, it can encompass the inclusion of units that had not been admitted previously, or the initiation of a communique to follow different procedures than previously utilized. The division executive, seeking to increase confrontation among his department heads, succeeds by issuing a divisional memo to all heads, except one. Or an executive succeeds by calling a meeting of his department heads, purposely refraining from notifying one or two of the department chiefs. The anticipated result is increased opposition. The means to that result has been alteration of the formal communication channels.

In addition to the formal channels, the informal communication network offers excellent opportunities for development of conflict stimulation. The informal channels are all those other than superior-subordinate, hierarchical controlled channels dictated by the organization chart. They include all loosely knit and ill-structured groups. By definition, any communication that does not follow the scalar flow is informal. Informal communications, better known as the grapevine, are loosely-knit passages of information. Where this information is not substantially supported, it can be classified as rumor.

Informal communications offer outstanding opportunities for the administrator to increase conflict. By carefully selecting the messages to be distributed through the grapevine and the individuals to carry them, the manager can increase conflict. He can purposely manipulate receivers and message content to add, negate, or make ambiguous the communications that are carried by formal means.

In summary, through the utilization of different formal patterns or by feeding the informal grapevine, deviations from traditional channels redistribute knowledge within the organization. And because knowledge represents power, modification of communication channels redistributes the power among organizational members.

Repression of Information

When the administrator holds back information, he again redistributes power. Information that members seek or require, when withheld, leaves the seekers less powerful. This redistribution stimulates conflict by increasing some individual's or group's power at the expense of others.

Repression is represented in varying degrees along a continuum. Repression describes all suppressed behavior from the extremes of complete withholding of information to merely directing communications that are in some way incomplete. The administrator who withholds all or part of pertinent communiques out leaves some units disadvantaged and increases opposition between the haves and the have-nots.

The action of an academic administrator who sought to redistribute power and stimulate conflict in his organization is an example of information repression. A new dean was hired by a New England state university from another institution in the west to direct the school's College of Business. Between the time the dean was selected and his official starting date, he made monthly visits to the campus to talk with the administration, the current department heads, and the faculty. An item of high priority to the new dean was a major reorganization of the school in order to disperse the entrenched, longevous positions held by the current department heads. Additionally, he recognized that several of the young faculty demonstrated considerable promise and were the key to the future of his college. Instead of sharing his ideas on reorganization with the current administrators in the College of Business, the new dean chose to present the ideas for major change to those younger faculty. The impact of withholding this data from the present power group was to redistribute knowledge and therefore power within the college. It became obvious to the faculty that a new power alliance was developing, fostered by exclusion of the current department chairmen from the planning of the new organization. As one would expect, conflict intensities were increased.

Transmission of Too Much Information

In contrast to repression, which transmits too little information, it is possible to increase conflict by clogging the channel with too much information. When overcommunication occurs, it becomes difficult to separate important factors from the superfluous. Confusion occurs, as does ambiguity. The manager seeking to stimulate conflict can utilize communication overload as an effective technique.

A head nurse implemented the information overload method when she envisioned her nurses becoming more robotlike and less professional in their nursing functions. She sought a method for halting a growing "Yes ma'am—No ma'am mentality" among the nurses. She wanted her staff to be concerned with changing and improving the functions they performed, rather than with their apparent total allegiance to the status quo. She interpreted many of the errors being made in the department to lethargic thinking habits. As professionals, she wanted them to be concerned with improving the services they performed, and this required more than just following orders.

The solution she initiated was planned communication overload. By transmitting a wealth of work related information through departmental correspondence and at departmental meetings, results could be seen within several weeks. She had awakened the thought potential of her staff, forced them to perceive the relevant factors from the data transmitted, increased the interaction between the staff and herself, and had the staff questioning the status quo and initiating the search for better ways to perform their duties.

Ambiguous or Threatening Information

Communications that are purposely designed to be ambiguous are separated, for our analysis, from those that create ambiguity. When channels become overloaded with information, ambiguity results, which creates conflict. When an administrator communicates ambiguous information, he directly creates conflict.

The administrator who seeks to increase conflict could, for example, initiate a memo to other units that is explicitly vague and unclear. The memo may implicitly have contradictions. This creation of an ambiguous memo will cause other units to reassess the communique's purpose, question the value of its content, and seek inconsistencies. Additionally, it can reduce the apathy in an environment that accepts, unchallenged, all communications.

As one might theorize, communications that appear to threaten will actively encourage conflict. Information that a plant will close, that a department is to be eliminated, or that a lay-off is to be incurred will rapidly accelerate conflict intensity. When one's survival is imperiled, either as an individual or through his unit, the trend of reaction is toward increased antagonism. When the communications indicate win-lose conditions the intensity of conflict will be further heightened.

STRUCTURE

Utilization of the structure of an organization is possibly the most effective way of managing the creation of conflict. By the way we group activities, we can inject both healthy and unhealthy conflict into the organization.

Because every organization possesses a formal structure, any change that results in redistribution of resources or power can be expected to increase conflict. The interrelationship between conflict and change is underscored in the area of structure. Through redefinition of jobs, altering of tasks, and reforming of departments, sections or total activities, previously established relationships are broken down. Conflict is increased as a result of fear among participants of uncertainty, of the displeasure of possibly having to assume or learn new tasks, or of possible loss of status. Therefore, by altering structural-relationships in the organization, it is possible for the administrator to increase interpersonal and intergroup hostility.

The nature of five specific structural factors will be discussed as conducive to initiation of conflict: size, bureaucratic qualities, leadership styles, position alterations, and interdependence.

Size

As established in earlier chapters, size can affect conflict levels. As organizations grow, conflict potential increases. A greater number of organization layers accompanied by increased specialization encourages separation, empire building, and selective perception. Accordingly, the administrator can stimulate conflict by increasing departments and divisions within the organization.

Discussion in Washington occasionally moves to the debate of whether the various armed services of the United States should be combined. At present the Army, Navy, Air Force, and Marines are each separate units under the Secretary of Defense. If these had originally been developed and maintained as one armed service, it could be postulated that conflict between the four service units, much of it constructive, would be significantly reduced. The design of the government to maintain separate units increases the potential for both competition and conflict, resulting in a more viable and responsive defense organization.

Bureaucratic Qualities

Increasing the number of organizational subunits will additionally reinforce specialization. As the organization expands, it relies more on highly specialized fields of departmentalized knowledge. Tasks are combined into activities, and the activities into departments. Departments expand, thereby increasing the expertise levels within the unit but further removing them from the other departments. For example, the division of work, in excess, can result in an organization's finance department having great difficulty in dealing with the marketing department. Each has become highly specialized, speaking its own jargon, and lacking comprehension of the contributions and problems of the other.

This process may explain one of the mysteries of organizational theory—the enduring power of large organizations. As has already been noted, as size increases, so does conflict. Additionally, as size increases the difficulty of coordination increases. But large size develops its own counter-balancing mechanism. Increased size, through greater specialization, builds in adaptability through conflict stimulation. While "coordinators" have historically sought to eliminate differences, they have basically succeeded in only alleviating dysfunctional opposition. Such functional attributes as challenging and questioning of other departmental objectives and activities, and the innovativeness and creativity of decision making are encouraged. In the final analysis, it seems likely that large, functionally specialized organizations have their own built-in survival mechanism— they stimulate conflict. This may additionally explain the high fatality rate of small organizations where managers have generally been more successful in eliminating *all* conflict, both dysfunctional and functional.

Leadership Style

Although it is difficult to separate leadership from the environment created by the executive group, it is nevertheless important to designate that leadership style can influence and stimulate conflict.

Leadership research demonstrates that no style is universally effective. What may be effective in one situation may be totally ineffective in another. The administrator may be the leader, a position that he has expanded from the formal authority given him by the organization. Or, the leadership role may be held by a nonadministrative member. The leader is therefore designated by his ability to influence other individuals in the group. Thus, to be a leader it is not necessary to possess formal authority. However, needless to say, every administrator should ideally be a leader.

The style of leadership utilized by administrators can be a conflict catalyst. By altering style, either within an individual or through interchanging individuals between units, the effectiveness of the leader can be altered. Further, by altering leadership effectiveness, it is possible to create various levels of hostility between members within groups and organizations.

Carried to an extreme, this view can be implemented by creating a "bullpen" of administrators with various leadership styles. A specific leader is selected depending on situational conditions. Of course, a more effective method would be to have existing leaders deviate their style so conflict levels can be altered without the necessity of changing leaders.

An example of how this might be implemented was demonstrated in a research section of a major urban hospital. It had been previously directed by an administrator who used a democratic approach. A new administrator, who believed it was his responsibility to make decisions and to "tell" his subordinates what to do, succeeded in moving a peaceful but static and ineffective research unit into a viable, creative department. On the other hand, we might hypothesize the improved productivity that would result when a navy procurement group, accustomed to strong, autocratic leadership, is assigned a new commanding officer who relies on a participative style of decision making within the group. Each of these changes in leadership style stimulate group interaction, increase conflict, and can result in more effective attainment of group objectives.

Position Alterations

Another technique for conflict stimulation is through modification of the relationships between members in the organization. Changing relationships, in this context, includes the adding, deleting, and transferring of organizational members. Specifically, it can mean injecting infiltrators, breaking up homogeneous units, redistributing decision-making authority, and increasing policing functions.

Just as change of the structure can increase conflict intensities, so can a change in group members. When implemented, group stability is disrupted through injection of a disruptive force into a previously stable environment. The outside infiltrator may be someone who is selected specifically for his differing views, background, or experiences. The infiltrator's impact may be only as an addition to a unit or as a replacement in a transfer. Additionally, this infiltrator may be the proverbial "devil's advocate," who though he shares similar views with other group members, is assigned the task to question, attack, inquire, and otherwise resist any homogeneity of views.

Communication and leadership have already been discussed as conflict stimulators. But both of these are closely associated with decisions, and especially the decision maker. Additionally, decision making is closely related to the structure of the organization. By directing our attention to the decision maker, another key conflict catalyst variable can be isolated.

If we substitute a different individual to make the decisions, it usually insures an alteration of the structure. In the formal sense, this is true. However, we are well aware that informal decisions are made throughout organizations every day. When the purchasing department allows line department managers to directly initiate any purchase order whose total does not exceed $50, it tacitly ignores the company requirement that purchasing initiate all purchase orders. Should the purchasing agent tighten up this loose procedure, he alters the person who makes the decisions. One should not be surprised to find, in this situation, that a tightening of the procedure would arouse conflict between the affected departments and purchasing.

All organizations have policing activities, and they are natural sources for exciting conflict. Most representative of individuals performing these functions are internal auditors, but additional policing is performed by accountants, quality-control inspectors, and any members who review the actions of others to determine if they are being performed to specific standards.

By increasing the responsibilities of the policing groups, by developing new policing groups, or by making present police actions more explicit and therefore more visible, conflict can be increased. While all organizations have policing functions and therefore inherent conflicts between the police and the policed, giving greater responsibility to these units shows formal acknowledgment of their existence and impact, which acts to raise hostility intensities.

Interdependence

The discussion in Chapter 5 supports the positive relationship between conflict and interdependency. When individuals or organizational units find themselves seeking a common scarce resource; that is, when one's gain is at another's expense, or where dependency is only one way, conflict will be stimulated.

The aggressive administrator can increase conflict intensity by augmenting the dependency between units. Requiring one department's activities to follow another's, such as on a long-belt assembly line, creates such a dependency. The development of a single fixed dollar budget, from which several departments allocate their individual departmental budgets, represents another incidence of created dependency. The fixed nature of the larger pool of funds creates a zero-sum game for the participating departments and stimulates conflict levels.

PERSONAL-BEHAVIOR FACTORS

Personal-behavior factors are the most difficult to manage. Any attempt to alter an individual's behavior is an ambitious task. Personal-behavior factors influence social conflict more indirectly than the previously mentioned stimulants. This is due to personal-behavior stimulants growing out of psychological conflict. Chapter 6 presented four factors that can effectively increase intraorganizational conflict: the personality characteristics of the leader, role requirements of members, status incongruence, and separate subunit goals. Each develops from intrapersonal turmoil, then spreads to the interpersonal level. A detailed discussion of each of the four was made in the earlier chapter, so only a brief review is needed here.

Leaders who possess the personality characteristics of high authoritarianism, dogmatism, and low self-esteem will stimulate conflict between organizational members and themselves. By utilizing popular personality and leadership questionnaires, it is possible to single out individuals within the organization who possess these traits. An individual with these qualities can then be moved into a leadership position, which will increase the probability of successfully stimulating intraunit conflict.

Individual group members who find the role behavior expected of them in their position disagreeable will stimulate intraunit conflict. A person in role conflict will project his or her internal opposition externally, therefore increasing the conflict intensity within the unit. The administrator

who is knowledgeable of his members' attitudes, can then heighten intrapersonal, and eventually interpersonal conflict by placing individuals in
positions where role expectations clash with personal beliefs and attitudes.

Stimulation will also occur if members perceive an incongruence between the status they discern in their position and the status that others
attribute to it. When the former is greater then the latter, member dissatisfaction and increased unit hostility can be anticipated. The administrator
can influence status perception considerably by his overt behavior toward
each of his organization members.

Such is the case, for example, when the district manager for the telephone company overtly accords different prestige grading to each of his
department heads. If each is acknowledged by the organization chart to
have the same formal status, such actions by the district manager to cir-
cumvent this parity should stimulate conflict. A previous feeling by the
department heads of general unconcern with their responsibilities may be
readily altered by the district manager's overt creation and demonstration
of status incongruence. From status incongruence, intrapersonal conflict
develops, which in turn emerges as interpersonal conflict between the individual or individuals in conflict and other department heads and the district manager.

Finally, interunit conflict is encouraged when the goals determined
by members of organizational subunits prove to be incompatible. Consequently, conflict levels can be stimulated by the manager's stipulation of
noncompatible goals and by withholding information. Each will result in
the development of inconsistent and conflicting subunit objectives. The
district telephone manager described above could also have reduced apathy
among his department heads by allowing them to set incompatible goals.
Assume the customer service department had set as one of its goals the
reduction of its direct labor costs, while the directory sales department,
which was a heavy user of the customer service's offerings, was seeking to
significantly improve its performance. But improved performance by directory sales will require increased labor cost for customer service. In this
example, the district manager will have increased conflict between the two
units by allowing the departments to set antagonistic goals.

SUMMARY

The suggestions presented in this section have represented a radical departure from previous treatises on conflict management. A new dimension
is added when conflict stimulation is recognized as an essential ingredient,
which necessitates developing methods for initiating and increasing conflict

levels. This chapter has suggested a number of these stimulation methods, certainly not as the final word, but as a catalyst to stimulate others.

The stimulation techniques presented are no more or less important than the resolution suggestions made in the prior two chapters; the key difference has been the depth of study. Whereas the material on resolution is considerably more comprehensive, it has been the purpose of this chapter to create a base from which conflict stimulation techniques can grow.

The next chapter will merge the suggested resolution and stimulation techniques with the multitude of conflict sources. The resultant model will create a workable framework for the contemporary administrator seeking to practice the interactionist philosophy of conflict management.

IV

MANAGING CONFLICT

The management of conflict can be conceived of as a process. The variables and relationships that make up the conflict management process have been described in earlier chapters. Now, it is necessary to integrate the earlier material and make it operational. These objectives can be achieved by construction of a model that accurately describes the conflict management process. Chapter 10 develops and describes such a model.

The final chapter briefly summarizes the interactionist philosophy and draws conclusions from the literature review. Also in Chapter 11, the future of conflict management is explored. Based upon the findings and analysis in the earlier chapters, these predictions seem logical and realizable. Generally, they support our belief that the study of social conflict will become the focal point in the study of administration and organizations throughout the 1970s.

10

Model

Development

The objective of this chapter is to synthesize the earlier discussion and to develop a comprehensive conceptual model that will describe the conflict management process. The discussion begins with the development and analysis of the model's three subparts: the Conflict-Intensity Continuum, the Planning-Evaluation Process, and the Choice-Action Increments.

CONFLICT INTENSITY CONTINUUM

The intensity of conflict can be conceptualized as a continuous range. Figure 10–1 depicts this range, beginning from a no conflict position and rising to conflict's highest state, described behaviorally as the act of destroying or annihilating the opposing party. This Conflict Intensity Continuum (CIC) includes all degrees of latent and overt conflict actions that exist between individuals, groups, and organizations, and within the latter two.

No attempt has been made to explicitly define points along the CIC, other than recognizing that any point above another is of higher intensity. The lower range might include situations where uncertainty exists over whether there is agreement among parties. The middle range could com-

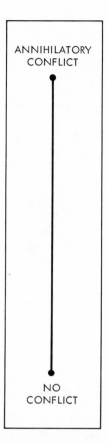

FIGURE 10–1 CONFLICT INTENSITY CONTINUUM

prise tense and anxious activity, open debate, and conscious and deliberate blocking of another's goal. The higher range would comprise openly aggressive acts, physical force where no permanent harm is incurred or intended, and ultimately annihiliatory behavior that aims to eliminate the opposition.

Figure 10–2 adds numerical positions to the CIC. This ordinal scale will facilitate in differentiating functional and dysfunctional segments and conceptualizing desired and actual conflict intensities. But when functional or dysfunctional conflict is defined by the CIC, it is extremely important to recognize that the reference is not to conflict actions or activities as it was in Chapter 3. Rather, the discussion concerns conflict *intensities*. In Chapter 3 functional and dysfunctional were defined from a micro perspective; that is, in terms of incidences. A particular activity was judged constructive or destructive by its impact on the organization's performance.

Now the discussion will be redirected to conflict intensities, which is

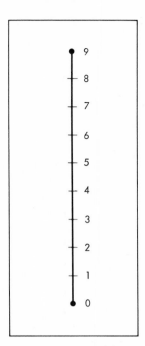

FIGURE 10–2   CONFLICT INTENSITY CONTINUUM—NUMERICAL

a macro view. The micro definitions would have described a debate between two executives as functional if it furthered the organization's objectives. An environment that, at a given moment, included four functional conflicts would have been interpreted as totally functional. This chapter will present a macro perspective in which, for example, four functional activities can cumulatively create a conflict intensity greater than desired and thus possess a dysfunctional segment. Conflict's functionality or dysfunctionality, at the macro level, which is the view taken throughout this chapter, is then determined by interpreting its intensity. Any *intensity* beyond the level sought will be destructive and dysfunctional.

By adding numerical positions to the CIC, it now becomes a tool for planning and evaluating the level of conflict intensity in all areas of the organization. The planning dimension is represented by the establishment of a desired intensity of conflict, whereas the evaluation dimension measures, compares, and takes corrective action where necessary. To illustrate, assume an administrator believes a conflict level of "3" will be most effective in attaining his unit's goals. He then takes his unit's conflict "temperature" by determining the actual level and compares it to the standard sought. If the actual measured level of conflict is "5", then resolution of the difference between "5" and "3" is needed, as depicted in Figure 10–3.

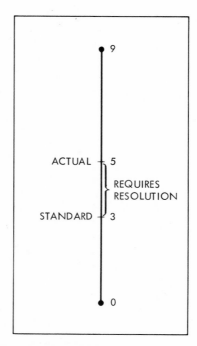

FIGURE 10–3   NEED FOR RESOLUTION

It is important to note that, in this example, the distance between "0" and "3" represents functional conflict; the distance between "3" and "5" being dysfunctional. We can define functional conflict then to be the distance between "0" and standard. The dysfunctional segment is the difference between standard and actual, when actual exceeds the set standard. As we will discover later in this section, the administrator will implement a resolution technique that will only reduce conflict intensity to "3", not to "0".

What if the desired standard is greater then the actual level? Let us assume the standard is again "3", but the actual is only "2", as shown in Figure 10–4. Functional conflict is represented from "0" to "3", as before. But now a greater degree of functional conflict is needed. Stimulators are required to move intensity from "2" to "3".

In the rare instance when actual and standard are in agreement, conflict intensity is at the optimum level. Conflict management then only entails maintaining the current conflict intensity, reviewing the standard to determine if it requires readjustment, and frequently assessing the status of the conflict to insure no deviations have developed between standard and

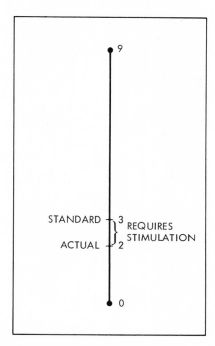

FIGURE 10–4   NEED FOR STIMULATION

actual. Where the two are in agreement, the desired state is being achieved, and all conflict is functional.

PLANNING-EVALUATION PROCESS

The CIC should be viewed as a planning and evaluation tool. It is not intended to be definitive, but rather instrumental in depicting the range of conflict and the relationship between intensities sought and those actually occurring. The Planning-Evaluation Process brings us again to basic administrative theory. As discussed in Chapter 1, administration includes the setting of goals, the review of performance in view of these goals, and corrective action if needed. Conflict administration requires the same.

Figure 10–5 describes the Planning-Evaluation Process. It begins with the establishment of conflict goals or standards (S). Just as an organizational unit has performance or service goals, it must also have conflict goals. But how are these conflict goals determined? The only relevant criterion must be the administrator's ability to ascertain the degree of conflict

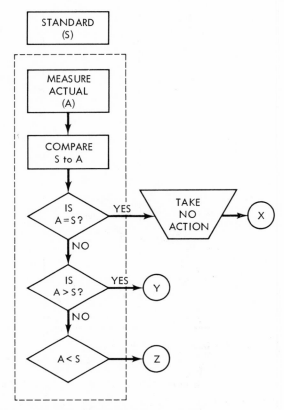

FIGURE 10–5   PLANNING-EVALUATION PROCESS

that will most effectively further the overall objectives of his unit. It is highly situational because what is supportive at one time or in one environment may shift dramatically at another time or place. Conflict goals then exist in a dynamic framework. They must adapt and change as the organization and its subunits adapt and change.

Two distinct parts are shown in Figure 10–5. Standards are separate to indicate this is part of the planning function. The remainder of the diagram is the evaluation process, which is shown as a dotted subsystem. The evaluation process is comprised of measuring, comparing, noting relationships, and initiating corrective action.

It is insufficient for the administrator to merely set conflict goals. Further efforts must be taken to assure that the stated goals are attained. This begins when actual (A) is measured. Determining the level of actual conflict is accomplished in the same manner that one ascertains if the standard level is being met—through the perceptions of the administrator. While no precise measuring instrument exists for measuring the organization's conflict temperature in cardinal terms, our earlier discussion of the

CIC as being comprised of lower, middle, and upper ranges, each with their rough definitional form, can be beneficial. From a pragmatic viewpoint, we need to direct our attention to only three questions: Is there deviation? Which way is the deviation? What is the degree of the deviation? To be any more specific, and therefore outline absolute measurable differences, is beyond the scope of this work. Further, it detracts significantly from our major objective; that is, developing a *conceptual* framework for managing conflict.

We now have two approximate measures—the administrator's perception of the current conflict state and an amount that he defines as the preferred state. The first key question now becomes important: is there deviation? The laws of probability tell us that some deviation will be found when we make our comparison. Therefore, a more workable definition of the A = S statement would be "Is Actual equal to Standard, *or within acceptable tolerances?*" If the comparison demonstrated parity at this point, there is no need to take corrective action, and we logically return to again review the situation for changes.

If there is deviation between standard and actual conflict intensities, then we need to ask: is Actual greater than Standard? If the answer is affirmative we go to Figure 10–6 and proceed from Point Y. If A is not greater than S, only one other alternative exists: A must be less than S. When this alternative arises, we will proceed along the lines shown in Figure 10–7, proceeding from Point Z.

The concern for the degree of deviation is considered in the Choice-Action Increment. The methods available for resolving or stimulating conflict vary in intensity. Therefore, the greater the deviation between Standard

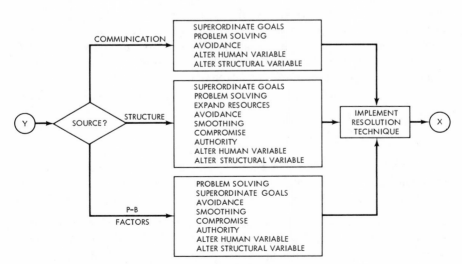

FIGURE 10–6 CHOICE-ACTION: RESOLUTION

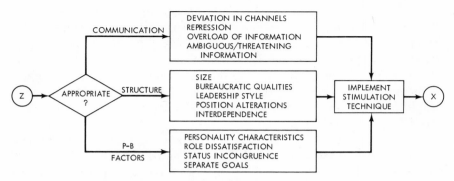

FIGURE 10–7   CHOICE-ACTION: STIMULATION

and Actual, the greater power or strength is needed in the stimulation or resolution method.

This concludes the detailed discussion of the Planning Evaluation model. We have set conflict standards, measured the actual conflict levels, made the comparison to determine if deviations exist, and initiated the first step to taking action where it is required. Let us now advance to the third and clearly the most complex subpart of the conflict management model—the Choice-Action Increments.

CHOICE-ACTION INCREMENTS

The final segment of our model is strongly laden with contingency variables. Figures 10–6 and 10–7 describe the process of determining the source of conflict and the applicable techniques for either resolution or stimulation, and then stipulates implementation. Figure 10–6 represents the selected decision process in those situations where resolution is necessary; that is, where Actual conflict intensity exceeds Standard. Figure 10–7 depicts situations where Standard exceeds Actual, thus requiring stimulation efforts.

Resolution Techniques

Conflict, as presented in Part II, can develop from inadequacies in three sources: communication, structure, or personal-behavior factors. Our model depicts this trilogy as the central part of Figure 10–6.

Communication.   The discussion in Chapter 4 described areas of distortion that can lead to conflict in communication. Specifically noted were semantic difficulties, insufficient exchange of information, and noise in the communication channel. The resolution methods suggested in Part III must be carefully scrutinized to find those applicable to reducing conflicts that arise because of inadequate communications. A brief review of these techniques will illustrate this point.

The expanding of resources would be irrelevant to a communicative conflict because scarceness is not a communication problem. Smoothing, compromise, and authoritative command are also inappropriate solutions to communication conflict. What is needed are techniques that will improve understanding and none of these methods can effectively achieve that end.

Only five of the nine techniques presented in Chapters 7 and 8 have relevance to communicative conflict: problem solving, superordinate goals, avoidance, and alteration of the human and structural variables. Let us briefly examine the manner in which each of these five can lower conflict intensity that is initiated by imperfect communication.

Problem solving is the most frequent and uncomplicated method used for resolving communicative conflicts. It is an open confrontation between opposing parties. Where conflicts have arisen due to ambiguity, distortion, the inadequate passage of information, or channel overflow, problem solving is a natural remedy. The major hurdle that must be overcome is getting the opposing parties to openly "communicate" about their communication problem. A newly elected city manager who publicly stated he would immediately implement improved garbage collection service found himself under heavy attack from the community as months passed and members of the community could discern no improvement in service. Upon investigation it was found that the community members interpreted "improved service" to mean more frequent pickups per week. The city manager, on the other hand, had meant earlier, quieter, and more economical pickups. As a result of a problem-solving session between the manager and a group of concerned citizens, the differences were uncovered and the city manager initiated action to increase pickup service from once a week to twice weekly. Efforts to economize and speed-up service were relegated to secondary importance. In this example, the city manager had only sought to meet the needs of his community, which he had interpreted as better garbage service. His definition, though, did not concur with that of his constituencies.

Superordinate goals seek to lower conflict intensity through development of a common objective, unattainable without the combined efforts of those parties involved in the conflict. Conflicts created by problems in communication will not usually be favorably affected by superordinate goals. The exceptions are those instances where lack of understanding can be improved through contact. Superordinate goals are effective in bringing people together and thus can create the opportunity for disagreeing parties to work together for a common purpose.

In the above problem-solving example the city manager resolved the differences between himself and the community through bilateral discussion. In some cases, the conflicting parties are not aware that their differences arise from problematic communication. In such instances, a third party, frequently a superior, can effectively promote problem solving. A wartime incident exemplifies this point. A new U.S. Army Captain had been assigned as a Company Commander. He replaced an officer who had demonstrated remarkable ability in protecting the lives of men under his command. The new captain attempted to convince his unit that a particular travel route along the marked roads was desirous, although the previous officer had advised his men never to travel the marked routes. The men of the unit would not follow their new officer's orders. After considerable frustration, the captain's superior initiated the resolution of this conflict by suggesting the captain and his men jointly confront the problem. The crux of the problem was found to be the men's respect for their prior commander's opinion and the prior commander's belief that the safest route in combat was avoidance of marked roads. Then, the new commanding officer was able to present information on why his suggestion was the best alternative and how the prior officer's dictum to always avoid marked roads had inherent weaknesses. The members of the unit, after this problem-solving session, understood the captain's reasoning. He had successfully presented evidence to allay their fears. The unit then accepted the officer's order to follow the marked road in pursuit of their objective.

Avoidance is a relevant but inadequate manner in which communication conflicts may be resolved. It is an applicable solution to any form of conflict, but its inherent weaknesses are obvious. Effective resolutions require taking a positive approach, not the defensive action of withdrawing from the confrontation.

The last two methods, altering structural or human variables, differ considerably from problem solving and avoidance due to the time that is required to make the resolution method effective. Structural and human changes are most often time consuming and therefore expensive. However, the value of such an approach is the permanence that results from a direct attack on the source of the conflict.

The impact of structure upon the communication process was detailed in earlier chapters. Formal communications are dictated by the authority relationships which in turn are determined by top management. The more complex the organization's structure, the greater the probability that communication conflict will arise: From Chapter 5, we can postulate that a multitiered structure, with narrow spans of management and therefore many administrative layers, will incur a greater number of communication problems than a comparable organization with wide spans of management and few levels from the operatives to the chief executive's position. Therefore, changes in the structure that alter the relationships between individuals can influence communication conflicts.

A final method for resolving conflicts arising from the ineffective transmission of meaning from one individual to another is to change the behavior of the conflicting parties. If the discord is due to ineffective speaking or listening skills, training to correct this behavior and the development of more effective skills should be considered. The cost and time requirements are high, and the possibility of being unsuccessful is significant, but when successful, the results are meaningful and of long-term value. Alteration of behavior focuses directly on the source of conflict, the communicator and the receiver, and thus can be extremely effective where this alternative is relevant and applicable.

Structure. Every resolution method discussed in Chapters 7 and 8 is applicable to conflicts developing from the organization's structural design. Structural conflicts can obviously be thoroughly resolved by altering and changing the relationships between members, but other techniques can be effective, if only temporary.

A structurally based scarceness of resource confrontation can be alleviated by making more of the resource available. While expansion of resources may create additional conflicts from peripheral parties not directly in opposition, it can be an extremely effective resolution tool. Problem solving and the use of superordinate goals can effectively reduce or eliminate conflict for the short or intermediate term. Problem solving may be more rapid in building a long-term resolution, but where it is necessary to alter attitudes, cumulatively reinforced superordinate goals may be significantly more effective. Avoidance, smoothing, and authoritative command have a major weakness in their failure to attack the source of the problem, but nevertheless they can be effective temporary techniques for resolving conflicts.

The use of compromise can be extremely effective in reducing structural conflicts. If the structure itself cannot be altered and the individuals within the structure cannot be changed to work more effectively and smoothly with internal incongruencies, then compromise can represent a meanful solution. In contrast to avoidance or smoothing, compromise offers a positive approach. Importantly, unlike authoritative command, compromise is free of win-lose consequences.

Our analysis supports the proposition that permanent resolution of structural conflicts is best achieved through change in the organizational structure. Where these changes cannot be achieved or entail costs that exceed their benefits, problem solving, the use of superordinate goals, or compromising tactics should be considered. The least powerful structural resolution techniques are avoiding and smoothing. Authoritative command can be a rapid and effective short-term solution, but its use must be accompanied by the expectation that conflict behavior will be evoked again from one or more of the parties who may perceive the authoritative decision to have been unfairly enacted upon him relative to the others involved.

Personal-Behavior Factors. With the exception of expansion of resources, the techniques presented for resolving structural conflicts also apply to personal-behavior factors. But, while the available resolution techniques are basically unchanged, their priority sequence for desirable results will vary considerably when compared to other conflict producing factors.

First let us determine why expanding resources is not relevant for these forms of conflicts. We stated in Chapter 6 that the major difference between structural and personal-behavior conflicts is that the latter is not within the influence of management. Personal-behavior conflicts are those that are inherent within the personality of the individual or individuals and therefore are not manageable. The alternative of expanding resources assumes a conflict over scarce resources, a commodity unrelated to personality factors and one that is obviously controllable by management. Therefore, this alternative is not relevant to personal-behavior conflicts.

Because personal-behavior factors emanate from the individuals involved in the conflict, rather than being external to them, the most effective method for conflict reduction is to alter the behavior of the conflict participants. Enough has already been presented pertaining to the difficulty of this undertaking, but in those instances where personal-behavior factors significantly deter from the performance of an organizational unit, this alternative should be carefully considered. The longer and more costly effort necessary to alter the ideas, attitudes, or values of one or more of the conflicting parties may be justified.

The most frequently used personal-behavior resolution technique is problem solving. The benefits and drawbacks of this method were described in Chapter 7 with specific mention made of the high regard in which it is held among both practitioners and researchers. Problem solving has major limitations when used to resolve personal-behavior conflicts. Differences that are generated as a result of internal attitudes or beliefs cannot be expected to change significantly in a single session where conflicting parties talk about these differences. One rarely changes his or her attitudes through confrontation. Numerous confrontations, or professionally conducted discussion sessions, may prove effective, but attitudes are long in developing and it would be most unusual to find them altered after a brief problem-solving experience. Therefore, while many administrators actively encourage "sitting down and having the disagreeing parties hash out the problem," the success of this method in resolving personal-behavior forms of conflict is questionable.

The use of authority is infrequently supported as an effective conflict resolver, yet it appears to have considerable value in the resolution of personal-behavior conflicts. Its value is not in its inherent strengths, but in its pragmatic successes. Realization that personal-behavior conflicts are difficult ones to correct at their source, creates awareness that while authoritative command may not reach the heart of the differences, it can be an effective short or intermediate-term weapon. In those cases where the time or cost required to correct a personal-behavior conflict is great, a resolution method may be necessary for the effectiveness of the organization, regardless of whether it is of a temporary nature or not. Thus, authoritative command can be a useful tool for the practicing administrator because of its ability to effectively reduce conflict intensity. Its lack of permanence is often acceptable when the alternative is no effective resolution.

As noted in Chapter 7, reinforced superordinate goals can successfully change attitudes held by an individual or group of another individual or group, therefore being an effective long-term resolution method. The difficulty is in finding workable reinforced goals. If the environment and the creativity of the administrator can provide these stimuli, superordinate goals can affect attitudes, and where they are serially reinforced, can successfully change behavior.

The remaining techniques each have significant limitations. Smoothing and compromise, like authority, are temporary solutions. Ignoring the differences, through the avoidance technique, does not actively seek a reconcilement. Alteration of structural variables is expensive, although a change in structure can be expected to influence attitudes.

Regardless of the method selected, the final step in the evaluation process requires the administrator to implement the resolution technique and return to renew the process again.

Stimulation Techniques

The Figure 10–7 decision tree has been reached as a result of an inadequate level of conflict. We stated in Chapter 2 that we no longer can accept the intensity of conflict within the organization as only either adequate or in need of reduction. A third choice, an increase in conflict, also is a viable alternative. Figure 10–7 assists in fulfilling this need by introducing the concept of stimulation.

When conflict intensity was excessive, it was necessary to determine its source. All conflicts are not alike and the selection and effectiveness of a resolution method is improved when we know the conflict source. As

Figure 10–7 shows, such is not directly the case with stimulators. While techniques work on one of the three sources, the administrator has greater freedom in selection of stimulators than resolutions. In order to increase the intensity of conflict, one needs to know its current level. Therefore, it is necessary to determine the source or sources of current conflict levels. But the key determinant is appropriateness. Organizational conflict can be intensified by using any of the techniques that the administrator believes appropriate. It may be a communicative stimulant, a structural intensifier, or a change in the personal-behavior factors that increases conflict.

While conflict intensity can be raised by application of any of the techniques, each technique possesses a unique power capacity. Because the degree of increase is important, this becomes a significant determinant. Some techniques are extremely potent, whereas others are mild. Some are directed toward temporary escalation of conflict, and others toward permanence. As we did with resolution techniques, our discussion of stimulators will be categorized according to source.

Communication. The previous chapter elaborated on potential ways to stimulate conflict within the organization. All the suggestions were made with the assumption that only if top management communicates its acceptance and seeks to develop an environment where conflict is encouraged, can the administrator control it. Therefore, all suggestions to expand conflict, shown in Figure 10–7, assume an environment in which conflict is tolerated and top management seeks the level of conflict that will optimize the performance of its organization.

Two particularly strong stimulators would appear to be repression of information and the communication of ambiguous or threatening information. Each is rapidly implemented and easily controlled. By holding back data we can quickly stimulate greater conflict. It can work as an excellent fine tuning device because the decision on the data repressed will influence the degree of increased hostility. Most important, it has an easily available escape valve should the intensity become too great and thus dysfunctional. A release of information should immediately initiate a reduction in conflict intensity.

Ambiguous information is very similar to repression. Ambiguity initiates discord, but the release of further information that can clarify the vague data will immediately set in action resolving forces. Threatening communications can succesfully stimulate conflict as rapidly as any of the techniques that we will discuss. When an individual's or group's survival is at stake, especially under win-lose criteria, conflict will rapidly accelerate. In contrast to ambiguity or repression, threatening information does not offer the easy safety valve. Perception is the key. When individuals are threatened, the actual removal of the threat may not reduce the hostility. If one perceives an action to be threatening, even though it no longer is, he will behave as if he is truly threatened. Therefore, the administrator who uses threatening communications to increase conflict must recognize that should intensity become too great, not only will the threat need to be rescinded but also the perception that the threat still exists must also be removed.

Finally, initiating changes in channels or overloading the channel with information offers opportunities for stimulating conflict. Deviating communication from previous formal channels and utilization of the informal grapevine are both effective, the latter being a frequently used method for disseminating threatening information. Through the transmission of too much information, channels can be overloaded, resulting in confusion and accelerated conflict levels. One weakness in utilizing channel overload would be the possibility of organizational members selectively filtering the information. The full impact may be reduced as individuals only absorb facts they view as relevant; receiving only the data they want to hear.

Structure. Figure 10–7 indicates five methods for stimulating conflict that relate to altering variables within or about the structure: size, bureaucratic qualities, leadership style, position changes, and interdependence. Let us look briefly at each.

Our analyses in Chapters 5 and 9 support the supposition that as an organization increases in size, conflict potential increases. By increasing the number of organization entities, the total organization becomes more complex and opposition is stimulated. Such actions are costly, therefore the decision to increase size solely to spur conflict would probably occur only when conflict intensity had reached a long impasse at an obviously inadequately low level. As the size of the organization expands, bureaucratic tendencies will be reinforced. Specifically, increased specialization will stimulate conflict intensity.

By altering his style of leadership, the administrator can influence conflict intensity. Erratic inconsistencies can be expected to initiate hostility. Movements, for example, back and forth between autocratic and democratic behavior could be expected to confuse organization members and stimulate conflict. Additionally, the use of participation was found to intensify conflict as high interactions solidified differences more than facilitating cooperation.

The administrator can further stimulate conflict by modifying the relationships between organizational members. By adding, deleting, or transferring employees, equilibrium of social groups is disturbed, thus creating and stimulating conflicts. Transferring into a unit a "devil's advocate," who seeks to challenge the traditional views of others, would be included here. Additionally, our finding in Chapter 5 that tenure and conflict appear to be inversely related, would support administrative efforts to infuse units with young individuals and to intensify conflict through increased turnover.

Finally, structural conflict can be accelerated by increasing the interdependency between individuals or organizational units. By organizing so as to create interpersonal or interunit dependency, especially one-way dependency, the administrator will stimulate conflict.

Personal-Behavior Factors. The third and final branch in Figure 10–7 proposes four methods of stimulating personal-behavior forms of conflict. As noted in our previous chapter, they generally lack the potency of methods previously mentioned.

Our findings indicated leaders who possess the personality characteristics of high authoritarianism, dogmatism, and low self-esteem stimulate conflict between themselves and their followers. As management, we can control the placement of individuals in specific positions; therefore utilizing administrators who possess personality characteristics conducive to conflict stimulation. While this represents an alternative, its success depends on finding an individual with these characteristics and, more importantly, the recognition that the result will be as much a function of the followers as it is the leaders. If the followers *expect* the three personality characteristics previously mentioned in their leader, conflict is more likely to be initiated by giving them a leader with considerably different qualities.

When a group member finds the positional role behavior expected of himself disagreeable, it can stimulate intraunit conflict. Also, stimulation will develop if members perceive a significant disparity between the status they discern in their position and the status others attribute to it.

Finally, interunit conflict is encouraged when the goals set by organizational subunits prove incompatible with other units within the organization. Administrators have the opportunity to stimulate conflict by stipulating noncompatible subunit goals and by withholding communications, which will result in inconsistent and conflicting subunit objectives.

Once the method or methods for stimulation are selected, the administrator must initiate the final step in the evaluation process. He must implement the stimulation technique and return to initiate the entire process again. We now can proceed to the final section of this chapter, which will integrate the three models we have already discussed into a comprehensive conflict management model.

CONFLICT MANAGEMENT MODEL

The final synthesis of our discussion on the management of conflict is depicted in Figure 10–8. It is comprised of our three conceptual models: (1) the Conflict-Intensity Continuum, (2) the Planning-Evaluation Process, and (3) the Choice-Action Increments. We can conclude this chapter by briefly following the flow of Figure 10–8.

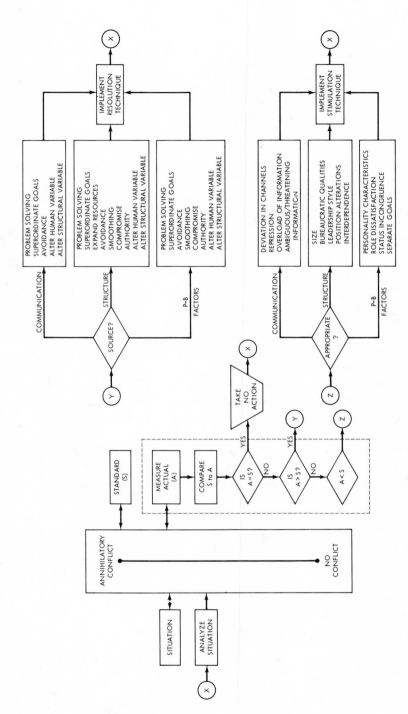

FIGURE 10–8 CONFLICT MANAGEMENT MODEL

109

A situational variable has been added to the CIC for the purpose of emphasizing that the administrator decides whether goals are being accomplished through his perception of the situation. Equally important is the recognition that the situation will affect conflict intensity and vice versa. The administrator's objective is to utilize conflict to manage the situation and therefore maximize effectiveness. He begins by analyzing the situation. From the facts that he has available he then utilizes the CIC concept to determine the level of conflict that he perceives will be most effective for his group or organization to achieve their designated goals. A conflict goal or standard is now established. The conflict planning aspect of the model is now complete and we are ready to evaluate conflict intensity.

The evaluation process is shown in Figure 10–8 as a dotted subset. It begins with the measurement of actual ongoing conflict intensity. This reading is measured along the CIC, as was the Standard. Once Actual conflict has been perceived and subjectively measured by the administrator in CIC terms, we must compare Standard to Actual. If they are equal, we have the desired state; that is, conflict exists in the amount necessary for the unit to optimize its performance. No action is necessary and we return to repeat analysis of the situation. A subsequent analysis of the situation may indicate that the Standard previously established is no longer the level that is most effective. Should this be the case, Standard will be adjusted and the evaluation process is repeated. Even if Standard is unchanged, the process is continually repeated as part of the closed loop system.

Our model tells us that if A and S are not equal, that two other alternative states exist: A is greater than S or A is less than S. If A is greater than S, we proceed to the Choice-Action Resolution Increment (Y); if A is not greater than S, it must obviously be less than S, and therefore we must go to the Choice-Action Stimulation Increment (Z). Note the logic of our flow because if Actual exceeds Standard, it must be reduced, thus the resolution increment. If Standard exceeds Actual, conflict must be increased and therefore we proceed to the stimulation increment.

If reduction of conflict is necessary, we need to determine its source. Given the source of the conflict, we can select and implement one of the relevant resolution techniques and return to again analyze the situation. The process is repeated for stimulation, with the exception that here greater options exist. The technique selected will be the one which is perceived as being most appropriate. Whatever action or lack of action is found necessary, it will be noted that the administrator always returns to the Situation. Since the Situation and conflict intensity interact upon each other, we recognize that our conflict management model is highly dynamic, with continual changes potentially occurring within the Situation, and thereby altering the desired level of conflict and the actual level within the group or organization.

SUMMARY

This chapter has integrated our knowledge of the administrator's role with the research on sources of conflict and methods available for resolving and stimulating conflict. Though the model is intended to be conceptual and not a "cookbook" approach to managing conflict, it presents a logical flow from which the administrator can rationally manage conflict intensity within his unit to improve his unit's performance. The *art* of managing conflict is still a critical determinant of his success. The ability to determine a planned level of conflict intensity is art, not science. So is the perceptual measurement of actual conflict. And finally, of course, it is the creative administrator who can accurately select the optimum technique or techniques and implement them in such a manner as to bring actual conflict intensities into alignment with those desired.

11

Recapitulation

SUMMARY

In the previous ten chapters we have sought to redefine the role of conflict in organizations. Our approach has heavily emphasized the positive side of conflict. Opposition has been shown not only to be desirable but also absolutely necessary for the survival of organizations. Conflict stimulates conditions that breed change. Change brings about organizational adaptation. Finally, through adaptation to the dynamic environment, and only through adaptation, the organization survives. Constructive conflict has been shown to be an absolute necessity for survival of organizational life, and survival is the primary objective of any organization.

The perspective taken by the author has been described as an interactionist approach. In contrast to the traditionalists who seek to eliminate conflict, or the behavioralists who accept its existence, the interactionist perspective encourages conflict. The dominant theme of this book has been to recognize the absolute necessity of conflict, to acknowledge the need to explicitly encourage its functional component, to redefine conflict management so as to include the stimulation dimension, and to emphasize conflict management as a major responsibility of all administrators. It has been the basic assumption throughout this work that only through acceptance of this interactionist philosophy can the administrator maximize the performance of his organizational unit.

Gaining acceptance of the interactionist philosophy was shown to be a difficult task because it runs counter to the ethos of most cultures. Specifically, we accredited the home, church, and school with reinforcing anti-conflict attitudes. A paradox emerges when we contrast cultural influences and needs of the organization. Our early socialization about the undesirability of conflict is constantly reinforced and is in contrast to the requirement for administrators to tolerate and often encourage conflict in the best interest of their organizations. Hence, the behavior that we deem necessary for optimum administrative performance is often difficult to achieve because we have been imbued with contrary attitudes.

Three specific sources of conflict were outlined: communication, structure, and personal-behavior factors. When we state $Ct = f(Cm, S, P\text{-}B)$, we have described conflict as a function of these three variables. A change in any one of them will affect the intensity of social conflict.

Resolution methods were described as techniques for reducing conflict intensity. Our discussion included nine alternatives, each possessing specific strengths and weaknesses. These methods were problem solving, using superordinate goals, expanding resources, avoidance, smoothing, compromise, authoritative command, and altering human or structural variables. Specific emphasis was given to the power of the technique; that is, whether it produced a short-term solution or actually got to the source of the conflict and produced permanent resolution to the particular opposition.

The totally new area of conflict stimulation was presented in Chapter 9. In contrast to previous treatises on managing conflict, stimulation was shown to be a significant tool of the conflict manager. The methods developed from the $Ct = f(Cm, S, P\text{-}B)$ model.

The last chapter outlined a conflict management model. Its purpose was to describe the conflict management process and give direction to the administrator. The model was comprised of three parts. The first segment was the Conflict Intensity Continuum, a conceptual device used to describe the breadth of conflict potentials. The second part introduced the management process, specifically the planning and evaluating of conflict intensity. Finally, the model was completed with the addition of the Choice-Action Increments, which outline appropriate resolution and stimulation devices.

In retrospect, we have sought to redefine conflict from an administrative perspective, analyzing its sources, and reviewing ways to increase and decrease its intensity. Working from a theoretical base, we have sought to develop pragmatic direction.

CONCLUSION

We can draw one major conclusion from this study: administrators must take the offensive and seek to manage conflict. We advocate an aggressive approach based on our belief that the cost of not managing conflict is too high to sustain. Obviously, this will compel administrators to accept the interactionist philosophy. Awareness and acceptance, followed by implementation of this philosophy, will increase our organizations' abilities to survive in the dynamic and ever-changing environments in which they operate.

Conflict management is not unlike the field of administrative theory in that both are comprised of science and art. We have presented a scientific framework for the study of social conflict in organizations. It should not be confused with a "how-to manual" for managing organizational conflict. There are numerous situational factors that severely limit our ability to generalize. These contingency variables are the key to successful conflict management. Herein lies the art of management: the creative ability of the administrator to ascertain desired and actual levels of conflict and to implement the proper method for aligning the two. Our discussion has not presented a panacea for organizational ills nor for correcting inherent weaknesses an administrator may possess. Understanding of the interactionist philosophy and our resolution and stimulation methods is insufficient to insure successful management of opposition. If the administrator is to succeed, he still must possess judgment and experience along with knowledge. We have developed a foundation for understanding social conflict from an administrative perspective. Hopefully, this can be rapidly expanded, but judgment and experience will always be beyond a writer's control.

While we provide no final answers in this text, we have refocused attention on the function of conflict in an organization. New directions have been given and general misconceptions have been clarified. The future acceptance of the interactionist's philosophy is up to you.

PERSPECTIVE

Any attempts to foresee the future are associated with high probabilities of failure. Though we recognize this fact, three trends appear probable enough to commit ourselves to prediction.

First, we can expect managers to increasingly accept conflict planning and evaluation as part of their roles. As long as these resource coordinators are measured on performance, we can expect them to accept the conflict management process as one which can be transformed into improved end results.

Second, the importance that conflict will play in the future study of organizations will accelerate dramatically. The bureaucratic model as a description of organizations will be displaced by the conflict model. We may expect to see increasing reference to a conflict approach to organization theory. Through a greater understanding of social conflict we will develop a more sophisticated analysis of organizational complexities.

Third, we can expect efforts to move significantly beyond our qualitative approach to measuring conflict intensity. Conflict behavior should be definable in quantifiable terms, and research to cardinally define conflict will improve our ability to manage it. The tools presented in these past chapters have provided rough guides. Quantitative measurement of conflict behavior would provide the administrator with highly desirable fine tuning capabilities.

The future of the interactionist approach to conflict management is bright. It has been our intention to focus the attention of the student of administration on managing conflict rather than to state eternal truths. Hopefully, researchers will find this work a stimulant to accelerate research in organizational conflict. Additionally, we hope it will motivate practicing administrators to empirically test and exercise the conflict management process and share their findings with us. To reiterate, the future acceptance of the interactionist's philosophy is up to you.

APPENDIX

Successful management has been described as a composition of knowledge, judgment, and experience. Each makes a significant contribution to administrative performance. While we have made considerable effort to develop the reader's knowledge of conflict management, we have done nothing to contribute to the enhancement of his judgment and experience in dealing with organizational conflicts. We need opportunities to test and apply the ideas that have been presented. This final section seeks to provide that opportunity for application and testing.

Both cases and interaction exercises require application of knowledge. They make some abstract ideas concrete, but each satisfies different needs. Cases are specifically designed to allow slow assimilation of facts, alternative development and analysis, solution selection and implementation. They develop analysis skills quite well, but only subordinately reinforce implementation.

It is one thing to have ascertained what you believe to be an excellent solution, but it is another thing to enact that decision. Interaction exercises are particularly effective for reinforcing an individual's ability to implement theory. Face-to-face involvement develops one's ability to rapidly react in a conflict environment. Therefore, the use of both cases and interaction exercises maximizes the development of the administrator or potential administrator's ability to use conflict stimulation and resolution techniques.

APPENDIX

Case Problems

CASE 1: UNBALANCED BOOKKEEPERS

The Central City Bank is the largest state chartered bank in the state. CCB boasts over forty-nine million dollars in deposits. It draws most of its customers from the upper-lower to upper-middle-class working groups. The bank itself is located in a predominately residential area with its main bank located in a shopping center. The main bank houses the installment, commercial, and mortgage loan departments, the personnel department, the auditing department, teller lines, safe deposit vault, and new accounts. CCB also has an Auto-Drive-in-Walk-in bank located five blocks from the main bank. The Drive-in Bank houses teller lines, safe deposit vault, new accounts, and the bookkeeping and customer service departments.

Whereas the Central City Bank opened about fifteen years ago, the Drive-in Bank has been in operation for only two years. The Drive-in Bank is managed by Dennis Oliver, an Operations Officer. Dennis is the only officer permanently based at the Drive-in Bank. Dennis has two supervisors working under him: Bernie Smith looks after the tellers and new accounts and Tom Stetson manages the bookkeeping and customer service departments.

Dennis Oliver was formerly in charge of the bookkeeping department before he was promoted to Operations Officer. Tom Stetson has been in charge of the bookkeeping department for ten months. Prior to his promotion to Bookkeeping Manager, Tom worked nights supervising proof operators. Tom attended college but did not graduate. He is friendly with most bank employees, but is known to be rather nervous and high strung.

The bookkeeping department is historically the bottom of the ladder in banking. Most bank employees start in this department. When you are a check filer, there is no way to go but up or out.

Tom supervises about twenty employees in all areas of bookkeeping. His subordinates are proof operators, check filers, customer service clerks, a return desk clerk, a messenger, and a central file clerk.

The operators who run proof machines must rerun each teller's work to check accuracy and then the operator routes the work through clearings. There are three proof machines in the department and the average tenure of each proof operator is two years.

Check filers are responsible for filing thousands of checks and deposits in the proper file, checking signatures for accuracy, and preparing the cancelled checks for monthly bank statements. The average tenure here is three to six months. These people must also answer phone calls from tellers who need to verify balances before cashing a check or processing a savings withdrawal. These people spend close to 50 percent of their time on the phone.

There are three girls working in customer service helping customers with problems. These girls have worked in the bank for at least a year and most have been in the community longer. The girl at the return desk has been in bookkeeping for nine months but is new at the desk. She is responsible for returning checks that are insufficient or not cashable for some reason. She works closely with Tom Stetson in deciding which checks are to be paid or returned for bank customers.

The girl in central file is responsible for keeping files in order. She changes addresses and cleans closed accounts out of the files and other similar tasks. She has been in central file for six months.

For the last six months Dennis Oliver has spent most of his time helping Tom in the bookkeeping department. This is because of a crackdown by top management on the large amount of write-offs and checks written with insufficient funds (N.S.F.). In the past, the bank has had a policy to pay a N.S.F. check rather than return it, except in cases where the account has a bad history. Tom has been under great pressure lately because N.S.F. checks have increased to nearly $1,500 per day.

The bookkeeping and customer service departments close at 5:00 P.M., whereas the operations areas of the bank remain open until 8:00 P.M. The night crew handles the greatest percentage of the bank's customers because most of the customers stop at the bank after work. Thus, the personnel in the new accounts area have to deal with many customers whose accounts have errors or discrepancies. Lately, many customers have complained that they are receiving the wrong checks in their bank statements. Additionally, some are complaining that they are not even receiving their monthly bank statements.

Another serious problem has arisen lately: established customers, with good accounts, are getting notices that their accounts are overdrawn. This is due to deposits not being posted. The result, needless to say, has been a growing desertion by good customers to other banks.

The personnel in the new accounts area are complaining to their supervisors about the number of unhappy customers with whom they are having to deal. Specifically, they are upset because the girls in bookkeeping make the errors, but they are the ones the customers see and at whom they take out their anger.

The tellers have started to complain to their supervisors because they must wait on the phone an excessively long time when calling bookkeeping for a balance. Tellers have had to wait as long as ten minutes to cash a customer's check. This makes the teller unhappy, but more important, it inconveniences the customers.

Mrs. Carr, the personnel director, has been plagued with complaints from employees in the bookkeeping department. They have expressed displeasure with the supervision they are receiving.

Most of the jobs in the bookkeeping department require little training or background in general banking and the workers find their jobs boring and monotonous. They also complain about the workload because the department is perpetually short of help.

The employees in bookkeeping are also complaining about harassment from their supervisors. They believe they are being punished for any mistake. They perceive their supervisor's behavior to indicate that he views them as unimportant. Tom Stetson is known to have a quick temper and the workers complain about his foul language. Most of the employees in the bookkeeping department have asked to be transferred, and a few have quit.

CASE 2: DANDY DIAPER SERVICE COMPANY

Bob Harris founded the Dandy Diaper Service Company (DDSC) in Flint, Michigan, twelve years ago. It was incorporated two years later, though Bob controls all the outstanding stock.

Bob began the business after serving two years in the Army, and although he was only 21 years old at the time, he borrowed $6500 from the bank to get the business started. DDSC was an immediate success. There was little competition for Dandy's service of providing diapers, delivered twice weekly to the home, washed and sanitized, for the busy mother. Dandy's competition could not compete with Bob's aggressive marketing tactics and quality service. Sales accelerated from $65,000 in the first full year of operation, to $180,000 in three years. More recently, total revenue and profits have been:

Year	Revenues	Profit (Loss)
1973	$157,300	$(16,800)
1972	178,800	(2,500)
1971	204,800	14,200
1970	222,700	17,500
1969	235,000	39,700
1968	240,600	47,500
1967	238,000	47,000
1966	235,500	43,500

Bob attributes the downturn "primarily to the introduction and rapid acceptance of disposable diapers, and secondarily to the decline in the birth rate." The decline in home delivered diaper business apparently is real. When Bob began the business there were three other competitors in Flint. A recent screening of the Flint Yellow Pages found DDSC to be the only home delivered diaper service listed.

DDSC currently has eighteen employees, in addition to Bob. This is down from a high of twenty-three in 1969. The layoffs have been viewed as a threat by many of the employees, creating what some employee's described as a "hostile environment." Bob volunteered that five years ago, "the organization was very efficient and employee morale was quite high." With the decline in morale has come increased activity by the Teamsters Union to organize the laundry plant personnel and the company's truck drivers. Bob Harris and his plant manager admit to fighting vigorously to keep the union out.

Key policy decisions are made by Harris, Larry King, and Dave Gibson, though according to King, "Harris runs the show." "Bob Harris appreciates others' views," said Dave Gibson, "but Larry and I both prefer not to inject our own opinions. Bob owns the business and it isn't our job to tell him how to run it. He pays us well and we do what is asked of us."

When King was asked about the unionization issue, he stated, "We have everything under control. Anybody we catch supporting the union will be fired on the spot. But if you quote me on that, I'll deny it!" Gibson, in response to the case writer's question of whether he was concerned about

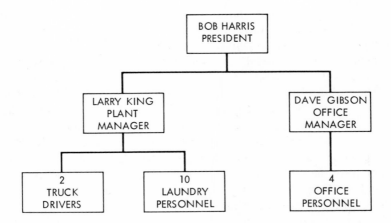

the drop in revenues and the two consecutive losses, replied, "Look, we're currently in a bind. Disposables are competitively priced and more convenient. We're charging $4.32 a week for six dozen diapers, compared with a package of 30 Pampers that sell from between $1.69 and $1.89 at markets and discount stores. It's difficult for us to do much. But things will get better. I think we've seen the end of the decline. Mothers will be returning to cloth diapers again."

When the case writer asked Bob Harris whether he was concerned with the decline in business, his voice rose. "Sure I'm concerned. But what can I do? I'm a little guy with a small business. The union is breathing down my neck, production efficiency has gone down the drain, and billion dollar corporations are putting me to the wall by marketing disposables. Do you know anyone who might be interested in buying me out?"

CASE 3: OFF SHORE DELIVERY

The Land-Sea Corporation is owned and operated by Jerry Benson. It is located in New Orleans and is a subcontract firm delivering supplies to off-shore oil drilling stations. The stations are found in the coastal waters of the Gulf of Mexico, but Land-Sea is concerned primarily with the tidewater stations off the coast of Louisiana. In addition to bringing equipment, Land-Sea brings food and other supplies on a regularly scheduled basis and is responsible for "short notice" cargo. Short notice cargo generally consists of critical items that are needed at the stations at times other than the regular weekly delivery.

About five years ago, Benson developed the idea of using an Army surplus landing craft (an LCM 8), a front loading craft, which is the same type that was used to deliver troops and supplies in the Pacific Island Campaigns of World War II. Benson is now using six of these craft to deliver the food and equipment for several of the major oil companies.

The major advantage of an LCM 8 is that it can be used without the aid of a pier and the other harbor necessities. It does not require a heavy lift crane because it is possible to drive a loaded truck onto the old landing craft, go to the off-shore station, and unload the truck directly from the boat. Formerly, many man-hours and considerable expense were incurred to accomplish the same task. The savings in capital equipment alone gives the Land-Sea Corporation a significant advantage over its competition, and has fostered the rapid growth rate currently being experienced.

Several newer companies are ready to assume Benson's contracts should he fail to produce the required services. The only contracts Land-Sea has received are on a "fill or kill" basis. That is, should the terms of a contract not be met, it becomes immediately opened for additional bids. Although the Land-Sea Corporation has been operating at a profit for the past four years, it is a very high risk business. A contract can be lost if a delivery date is missed by one day over the two day allowable grace period. As with most high risk operations, the prospect of profit is also high. Benson is continually revising and up-dating his operational procedures. Once he paid an employee a $300 bonus for devising a small hand operated crane that allowed cargo to be loaded over the side of the craft as well as from the front. This reduced the loading time for oil drums by one hour per load.

Benson uses very high employment standards and enjoys very low personnel turnover. To be employed by Land-Sea affords a certain amount of local status. The jobs offer high pay, plus a liberal bonus plan. In five years of continuous operation, Benson has fired only four employees, one of which was later rehired. There has been no evidence of racial prejudice brought to Benson's attention, although 30 percent of the seventy man work force is black. In addition to the blacks employed, there are several Mexican-Americans. Generally speaking, Land-Sea appears to offer a favorable work environment. Benson takes pride in knowing each of his employees on a personal basis. This relationship probably was significant in the employees' rejection of a unionization attempt several years ago.

Four of the six LCM 8s are in constant operation. But being WW II surplus, they are beginning to deteriorate from age and use. Although the hull and superstructure of each craft is fully seaworthy, the engines and related systems leave much to be desired. During the past few months the time required for routine maintenance has doubled. Replacement parts too, have been difficult to find. But possibly the most difficult task facing Benson is locating and training competent personnel to perform the maintenance operations. Last month, a decision was made to replace the entire fleet with larger, more modern craft but there is a six month lead time until delivery. In the meantime, it is critical for the survival of the Land-Sea Company that its remaining fleet perform adequately so the firm's commitments can be met.

But personnel trouble is apparently brewing. Jeff Logan, a white, has been with Benson since Land-Sea was formed. Thirty-five years old and a father of three, he is an exceptionally skilled machinist and mechanic. Logan had been the coxswain (driver) of an LCM 8 while he served in the Army and it was there he met Benson and the two of them initiated the idea of going into business. Logan declined a full partnership stating he "couldn't wear no white shirt." He did accept Benson's offer of a substantial profit sharing program, although he receives a bonus payment under the same criteria as the other employees.

Logan has been an effective teacher and trainer for Land-Sea. When a new man comes on the job, Logan works with him until the new man is ready to join a regular crew. It was Logan who personally organized the maintenance shop, utilizing former operator/mechanics as specialized mechanics. Among the older employees there is no doubt that Logan is the "second in command" at Land-Sea.

Bill Washington is coxswain of one of the landing craft. Thirty-two years old, Washington is black, married to a Panamanian girl and they have five children. He has over eight years' experience as an operator/ mechanic for the Coast and Geodedic Survey Teams off the coast of Panama. His qualifications are impressive and he was hired by Benson immediately following his initial interview. Washington's work record at Land-Sea is good. Although he has been late a couple of times, there has been no need to dock his pay, although there is company policy to this effect. Washington generally works well with the other personnel and is recognized as an expert in the field of amphibious operations. Many of his suggestions have been tried by the company, most with considerable success. On an occasion when one of his suggestions failed, Washington was quick to place the blame on the equipment and the improper implementation of the idea. He is bright and does not hesitate to take issue with Logan over any controversy that arises.

Washington also acts as the self-appointed spokesman for both the black and white members of the landing craft crews. Once, during an argument over proper loading of a craft, Logan relieved Washington of his responsibility and reassigned him to the maintenance shed. In Benson's operation this did not mean a loss in pay, just a slight loss of prestige. When Logan told Benson what he had done, Benson concurred. One week later Washington went in to see Benson, without going through Logan, and asked to be allowed to return to the landing craft as an operator. Benson tentatively agreed, contingent upon Logan's concurrence. When Benson contacted Logan, Logan agreed to take Washington back as an operator. Several months have passed without any further incidents.

Last week a tropical storm damaged several of the off-shore drilling stations. The oil companies began making immediate requests for the delivery of personnel and equipment to prevent a major oil leak or fire disaster. One of Land-Sea's crafts was in extended maintenance and could not be committed, but the remaining five were put into immediate operation to meet the urgent requirement.

The storm occurred on Monday, and on Wednesday morning about 9:00 A.M., Benson was in his office when Logan and Washington came busting through the doorway. Logan was upset and requested that Washington be fired on the spot. Washington, in turn, levied charges of racial prejudice and stated that if he went, "all the blacks will go with me." Washington told Benson that Logan has been "working me harder than anyone else in the company," and that racial slurs had been levied against him. Logan denied the accusations and stated again that he did not need Washington working for him. As Benson was listening to the claims and counter claims he heard two semi-trailer trucks drive into the receiving yard and knew they contained the food and supplies for Oil Station Five, a contract already one day into its grace period. He also knew the company was short of personnel.

CASE 4: SIX PLANT MANAGERS IN THREE YEARS

The case writer was plant manager for Maiden Industrial Service in Omaha, Nebraska, for one year while attending night classes at the local university. Maiden Industrial is an industrial laundry, supplying towels, walk-off mats, uniforms, dust cloths, windshield cloths, and other cleaning items to customers within a 260 mile radius of Omaha.

Maiden Industrial Service is a company of four industrial laundry plants; one located in Omaha, one in Grand Island, Nebraska, and two in Texas. The company is owned exclusively by Mr. G. Temple Dexter who maintains his office at the Omaha plant. Mr. Dexter is from a wealthy Chicago family. He never finished college but was left with a sizable inheritance when his father died. Mr. Dexter took his inheritance, entered the industrial laundry business, and built the present company completely on his own.

Every plant has the same formal organization as the Omaha plant. The lines of authority run from the owner, Mr. Dexter, to the district general manager, departmental coordinator, plant manager, and section foremen. The plant manager, sales and service manager, and office manager report directly to the departmental coordinator.

The plant manager is held directly responsible for coordination of plant activities, production schedules, training of plant personnel, supplies maintenance, record keeping, payroll, and security. The plant is divided into six sections: cotton uniform wash section, pressing section, synthetic uniform dry clean section, grease and ink towel wash aisle, regular industrial wash aisle, and packaging and assembly. Seventeen route trucks unload incoming laundry at the east docks. The articles are sorted and cleaned while they are moved through the plant and assembled for delivery at the west docks.

Five plant managers had preceded the case writer during the last two years. The immediate predecessor had said during the writer's three week training period that there was "too much for any one man to do." He advised on concentrating in just two areas: "meet production schedules on time and correctly calculate the weekly gross pay of each plant employee for the Saturday afternoon payroll reports."

It soon became clear that the plant management problems were seriously exacerbated by three important factors: the quality of the plant employees, the routemen, and Mr. Dexter himself. The plant was intentionally located in a ghetto area for the purpose of having a ready supply of inexpensive labor. The plant manager had fifty-six employees under him. Seven employees were high school graduates. These seven were section foremen and boiler room workers whose duties included planning, section supervision, and the actual operation of the more sophisticated equipment both in their respective sections and in the boiler room. These seven men were fairly well paid and responsible in their duties. The forty-nine remaining employees were paid the minimum wage regardless of responsibilities. Thirty-eight of the forty-nine minimum wage employees were women.

A yearly turnover rate of 60 percent for plant personnel was not unusual. Many of the women would work only two or three weeks to earn pocket money and then quit. Over a third of the plant manager's time was spent training new employees and updating records because of this extremely high turnover rate.

At times, to maintain the production schedules, any warm body that walked through the front door would be hired. Even employees that had been fired only a month before had been rehired when they reapplied for employment. The employees knew that management was in desperate straits, so they took advantage of the situation. The absenteeism rate reached 25 percent on some work days that, when added to fighting, stealing, goofing-off, drinking, and drug abuse during working hours, created quite a chaotic organization. Mr. Dexter believed that the only solution to the employee problem was the increased use of automation. He would not listen to or consider other suggestions or possible solutions.

The work environment and quality of the minimum wage employees perpetuated endless related problems. So much of the plant manager's time was spent training new employees that the fulfillment of his other duties began to deteriorate. Finally, he placed more training responsibility of new employees on the section foremen who reluctantly agreed to do the best they could. However, they allowed the training to deteriorate to the level of turning loose a trainee with the other section employees and hoping the trainees would learn enough from them. This method kept the trainees out of the foreman's way, so he could concentrate on other duties, but this so-called training produced increased inefficiency and higher accident rates.

The plant manager found he now had more time to concentrate on his other duties and to scrutinize the problem areas more closely. The biggest problems were trying to meet production schedules and attempting to sort all materials according to route so that everything would be placed on the correct trucks. The routemen were always short of uniforms, towels, or some other item, and they would come directly to the plant manager for a solution. The assembly department felt they were doing fairly well if they got 90 percent to 95 percent of the routes sorted and completed; but 100 percent completion was necessary in this highly competitive service industry in order to keep customer complaints to a minimum. No route was ever completely assembled and ready for delivery on time during the one year that the case writer was with the company.

The routemen were paid a good salary plus a commission on their service contracts. This correctly motivated them to give their customers good service. The routemen wanted all of their materials clean and ready for delivery on time. Since this was rarely the case, occasional cancellation of customer contracts occurred.

The routemen felt the plant manager was responsible for any shortcomings they discovered in the assembled laundry so they came to him with their complaints. He would go through the entire plant with one routeman after another searching for missing uniforms or other material. Occasionally one would find some of the missing items, but not very often. The paperwork would be reviewed to check for repair orders, replacement orders, or cancellation orders, and occasionally in the orders would be found the reason for the missing items. A copy of these orders could have been sent to the routemen, through the sales office, but this was never done.

The only reasonable conclusion that could be reached for the constantly disappearing material was employee theft. The routemen did not seem to care why the necessary items were missing. They wanted the missing material, usually shirts and trousers, on the truck and ready for morning delivery. The routemen knew this demand was impossible for two reasons. First, the assembly department finished work every day at 3:00 P.M., and the routemen never returned to the plant before 4:30 P.M. Secondly, new stock and replacement stock could not be issued from the storeroom without signed forms from the office. The office always took two days to issue the forms authorizing replacement stock for the routes. The routemen knew of this arrangement but they frequently sought out the plant manager to avoid the procedure, and be able to complete their next day route deliveries. Many of the routemen believed that if they yelled loud enough and long enough that what they needed would somehow be produced.

The antagonism increased greatly between the routemen and the plant manager when accidentally the manager discovered one of the routemen stealing uniforms and towels from the plant. He was reported and promptly fired by Mr. Dexter after a very brief investigation. From that moment on, this case writer was regarded by the routemen collectively as an enemy.

The quality and attitudes of the minimum wage employees in the plant and the demands made by the routemen created many problems for the foremen, but these problem areas were of minor significance when compared to the policies and practices of Mr. Dexter. The company was organized along formal lines of authority and responsibility, which the managers and foremen followed efficiently. Orders would come down the line and be executed promptly. But in almost every instance, the order would be revoked or corrected by Mr. Dexter personally. He rarely went through his managers in order to do this. Instead, he would storm into the plant, stand nose to nose with his object of wrath, and scream his correction or new decision at his victim. His victim could be anybody: plant manager, section foreman, or hapless employee. These almost daily scenes created such confusion and frustration that the foremen decided to ignore all office directives until they had an opportunity to talk with Mr. Dexter and receive his personal blessing.

On several occasions when Mr. Dexter was out of town, the case writer noticed that the plant functioned more smoothly and efficiently. There appeared a definite lifting of spirits among supervisors and operators alike. The case writer tried several times to make Mr. Dexter aware of the damaging effects of his random outbursts, but to no avail. Every suggestion, comment, or opinion relayed to Mr. Dexter was invariably met with his crisp stock speech. "Look, I'm paying you to be plant manager. Do the job. You got problems with employees and routemen? Take care of them. And when I see something wrong I'll handle it myself. So I'm actually helping you do your job. So don't complain."

CASE 5: UNITED MANUFACTURING COMPANY

United Manufacturing Company is a closely held, family corporation located in a small midwestern town of about 7,000 people. It employs 1,000, of which 50 are administrators and the rest shop employees. The shop is divided into fifteen departments with each department responsible for a different product. Each department has a department head and one foreman.

United has been very profitable the last five years, earning over 20 percent on sales. This profitability corresponds to the length of time the piece rate incentive plan has been in effect. United has a Wage and Salary Department and employs well trained industrial engineers to analyze and improve production methods, standardize operations, and set time standards for operations. Base rates for every job are bargained with the union, but management sets the piece rate and uses past performance as one criteria along with time studies.

In the incentive plan, the earnings of the employee are directly proportionate to his output. For every 1 percent increase in output, the worker is given a 1 percent increase in wages. In the past few years, wages have risen steadily to the point where they are high for their type of industry, and the highest in that immediate part of the country. The plant has a record of good labor relations. Turnover and absenteeism are also low.

One of the 15 departments is Department 551, which makes electronic relays that are added to the final product in the later stages of production. These relays are also sold throughout the country to other manufacturers in the same line. This accounts for approximately 25 percent of United's profits.

Six months ago a time study was initiated by the Wage and Salary unit of activities in Department 551. Although they told no one, word spread quickly throughout the department. Absenteeism soared from 5 percent to 20 percent. Employee concern was visible through a large increase in Department 551 grievances.

The Wage and Salary unit, on the basis of past performance and their time study, made the recommendation to top management that a new procedure be instituted in Department 551 that would make the job less complicated. At the same time, they recommended that the piece rate standard be raised. This effectively increased the standard approximately 15 percent. Top management accepted the recommendation and sent a directive to Fred Wilson, the Department Head of 551, ordering him to initiate the change. Wilson carried out the request and posted the new piece rate standards on the departmental bulletin board. The foreman, who aligns himself with Wilson, made sure the workers followed the new procedure by spot checking each worker five or six times a day during the first month and more recently, two or three times a day. He also counted the output of each worker and reported this to Wilson at the end of each week.

But the change is affecting production and worker pay. Until six months ago, the employees in Department 551 were averaging ninety dollars a month incentive pay and working at approximately 50 percent above standard. As soon as the Wage and Salary people started their time study, production dropped to 20 percent above standard and incentive dropped proportionally. When the new procedure was introduced and the new standard announced, production dropped initially to 70 percent of the former output. This rose steadily to 85 percent, but has stagnated at this level. Management attributed the initial drop to the new procedure but could not see why it did not rise again to the old level. The Production Department Manager believed some workers might be "holding back" production and instructed Wilson to fire anyone found "restricting" production. This led to the threatening of three top producers. Although their individual output went up, the department still averaged only 87 percent of the old standard.

Following the threat of discharge to these three men, grievances nearly doubled for the week and continued at 50 percent above normal for the remainder of the month. The shop steward that handled these grievances was very aggressive, and management believed he was partly to blame for the dissent. On the other hand, workers obviously felt he was representing them very well, as he had just been re-elected for his fifth consecutive six month term as steward. Most of these grievances were being directed at the new standard. The foreman's response has been to demonstrate to the workers who complain that the standards are easily attainable. He has done this by taking over a job and working fervently for about ten minutes; then announcing that he has no trouble meeting the standard.

Things have grown worse during the past few weeks. The employees of Department 551 have started wearing black arm bands and at times have worn their employee number pinned to their backs, in prison fashion. On these occasions they have marched up and down the aisles yelling at each other. On one occasion, about thirty people sat in the cafeteria until the precise time they were to return to their jobs. Then they jumped up, in the process knocking over chairs and spilling trays to the floor, yelling in unison "GO! GO! GO!" and marched out the door counting cadence. This obviously upset the entire cafeteria, which had about 200 people in it at the time. One startled man suffered a mild heart attack and was taken to the hospital.

Another time, 50 employees from Department 551 brought toy whistles to work and blew the whistles all the time they were at their desks. The foreman took all the names of those involved and turned the list over to Wilson. This list eventually reached the president of the company. The rumor around the shop is that the president intends to "dock" all the employees involved.

Lately, the workers in 551 have resorted to much more drastic tactics. One day they all sat at their work benches with their arms folded and refused to work the last hour of their work day. On another day, they all walked off the job at noon, after one of the workers got into an argument with the foreman. They have also taken out a full-page ad in the local newspaper accusing United of unfair labor practices.

Management is becoming increasingly alarmed about the turn of events. Sympathizers from the rest of the company are growing in number and the grapevine is carrying the report that if the workers in Department 551 call a strike, 60 percent of the other employees will follow in support. Production in Department 551 has reached the level where they are no longer supplying enough relays to fill the needs of United, much less the demands from outsiders. Also, because the employees took out the newspaper ad last week, several prominent businessmen from the area have inquired into the matter.

There are also other factors to consider: (1) the general economy is strong, with nationwide unemployment at a low 3.5 percent, (2) the local unemployment rate is only 1.8 percent, (3) and it takes approximately four weeks to train a person to do the job in the Department 551, with another eight to ten weeks wait before they normally reach 80 percent efficiency.

CASE 6: CHANGE IN DEPARTMENT THREE

Arco, Incorporated is a computer parts company located in the middle west United States. It handles over 20 percent of the region's parts contracts. Its present plant facilities utilize an assembly area involving twenty separate departments, and a highly technical area that handles the heavy construction material.

Arco is in the process of installing new plant equipment capable of cutting production time by 5 percent and increasing finished product lines by 10 percent every six months. The new facilities will revamp three of the assembly areas. Each of these three areas were notified 6 months ago of the new change. The members of each department were sent preliminary material on how the equipment functioned and each was instructed to attend a short meeting to be held one department at a time.

Department Three consists of one general foreman, three grade II operators, and three grade III operators. Bill is the youngest in his department, a 22 year old grade III operator. He is married and has one child. He is liked by most, well-mannered, seldom tardy, and has missed only two days in the four years he has been with Arco. Bill has worked hard to garner a working knowledge of his department, which is one of the more complex units in the company.

The men of Department Three are on a higher pay scale than most of the other departments, and the thought of an even more complex job made things look quite promising to the department's members—a higher pay scale, more job security, and a new and interesting approach to their tasks.

But while the men of the departments were anxious, they were also fearful of what was going to happen. They knew they all worked well together under the present system and the new, more complex, untried system made them eager but uneasy.

The plant supervisor and the department foreman presided over the meeting to discuss the change. They passed out up-to-date material on the equipment and explained the procedure that would be used to start production in the new department. While the starting date was six months away, full co-operation and interaction was asked. To work in Department Three, it would be necessary to attend a four week in-depth school and to complete an oral and written exam. Half of this class time would be spent actually working with the new equipment. It was explained that the department would be staffed with one foreman, two grade II operators, and two grade III operators. According to management, the two individuals who did not quality for the department would be transferred to another unit, not necessarily requiring the same grade skill, but as close to the present pay scale as possible. Further, it was stated that seniority would make no difference, for the operation was much too complex to use it as a criteria. The most qualified would be assigned the job. It was also explained that no other departments would be qualified, for it was believed that the skills in Department Three's operation were the closest to those required in the new tasks. Each man would be given the opportunity to achieve any of the grade II or III jobs. The supervisor stated that they did not want to eliminate these jobs, but the new system was operable only with the five men, and there were no other feasible alternatives.

The hot topic for the two weeks prior to the beginning of school was how the school would be run and the degree of difficulty for qualifying in the new job areas.

Bill usually eats lunch with the other men. Recently, during lunch, he opened the conversation with some angered comments concerning the breaking up of the unit and then began talking about how a change in positions might make it necessary for him to take on a part-time job. He volunteered that his wife was expecting, which put an additional financial burden on his family. His co-workers and friends followed Bill's remarks with some of their own comments on how a change to another job would affect them and their families.

The workers were becoming very conscious of each other and short quarrels and criticisms developed. The men were obviously tense. The supervisor and foreman asked the men separately what was bothering them. When Bill was asked, he replied that he was very concerned about his future and his family, especially with the new change coming. He expressed his concern over not having as much experience as the other men at his level, and his belief that he would not have a fair chance at getting assigned to one of the jobs. He felt the present unit worked effectively together and breaking-up their team would affect the new group's cohesiveness and performance.

The school began on schedule and right from the beginning Bill exhibited considerable enthusiasm. His goal was clearly to pass all the qualifications and get into the new unit. He attended classes regularly, participated actively in all the sessions, and often led the discussions. He asked and answered many questions. It surprised many of his co-workers that he was so intelligent, energetic, and alert to all the ramifications caused by the change. During lunch sessions Bill always talked favorably about how the unit could still work together well as a team.

But Bill still expressed reservations concerning his chances of being accepted. The men in his department did not share his view, although they did concur that seniority could not be totally ignored.

Bill soon realized from the apprehension of his co-workers that he had been mistaken in feeling he had little chance to get a position in the new department. In fact, he recognized he was doing extremely well relative to his classmates. But the once close ties between Bill and his co-workers seemed to be slowly deteriorating.

Department members grew increasingly vocal in expressing their desire to not be the one shifted to another department, yet at the same time they did not feel good about someone having to step out of their unit, just because of some "new fangled" equipment. The discussions eventually led to the subject of Bill. The departmental consensus was that Bill might even have a chance for one of the Grade II operator slots. They began to overtly show their concern that a younger department member, with fewer years in the company, might be moving ahead and taking one of their slots. The more the subject was pursued, the deeper their resentments became.

Halfway through the schooling period, one could discern a noticeable difference in the attitude of the entire group. Almost as if there was an inner pressure retarding progress, the members of the class worked hard to make each other look good at Bill's expense. The group seemed to be more concerned with attacking Bill than pursuing the subject matter.

When the time came for the oral and written examinations and for the trial run on the equipment, all of the members of the group scored below average, except Bill. The men obviously were considerably interested in who would be let go and who would stay. The group generally reconciled their low performance to pressures in class that impeded their study. They were unable to explain Bill's superior performance.

After conducting individual discussions with each of the men, the supervisor discovered that Bill had a just reason for his exceptional work. His young daughter of two years was undergoing necessary physical therapy to correct weak muscle tone from birth. It was extremely expensive and treatment was necessary every other week for the next year or so. If he were to be demoted to another department with a reduction in his current pay scale, he would be unable to meet the bills that had already accumulated nor afford future treatments for his daughter.

Management decided to extend the schooling for an additional two weeks, in order that test performance might improve. After only a day or two into the extended period, it became obvious that the participants were not responding. The result was increased pressure from the foreman and supervisor. It was made clear to the men that if they were going to take a passive role in getting into the new department, other alternatives would be used to get the area started into production. For example, other departments could be screened for approximate skills, or the tests could be eliminated and past performance used as the selection criteria. Whatever action is taken, the new equipment would have to be in full production within ninety days. At the moment, only Bill met the standards to operate the new equipment.

Interaction Exercises

EXERCISE 1: MANAGEMENT OF STRESS *

Goal

To establish a stressful situation in a group, in order to generate data about the resolution of tension, anxiety, conflict, and stress.

Time Required

Minimum of one hour.

Process

The facilitator suggests that the group might engage in an activity designed to promote stress in the group in order that members might focus on how the stress is managed. Several suggested designs are given.

* Source: J. William Pfeiffer and John E. Jones, *A Handbook of Structured Experiences for Human Relations Training, Vol. I* (Iowa City: University Associates Press, 1969), pp. 71-72.

After the group has completed the activity, a discussion of the process is held.

Suggested Experiences

1. Have participants form a line in which they position themselves in order of influence in the group. Include staff, and insist that the group complete the exercise. Discuss.
2. Within a strict time limit, have the group create a rating scale on the dimensions of leadership.
3. Have each group member choose a mother, father, brothers, and sisters from the group members.
4. Have the group create its own stressful task by establishing an ambiguous, leaderless situation.
5. Have each group member eliminate one other member from the group.
6. List all possible pairs of group members and rank order the pairs on similarity.
7. List all possible triads in the group, and in each triad find which two participants are different from the third participant.

EXERCISE 2: NASA EXPERIMENT *

Goals

I. To compare the results of individual decision-making with the results of group decision-making.

II. To diagnose the level of development in a task-oriented group.

Group Size

Between six and twelve participants. Several groups may be directed simultaneously.

Time Required

Approximately one hour.

* *Source:* J. William Pfeiffer and John E. Jones, *A Handbook of Structured Experiences for Human Relations Training, Vol. I* (Iowa City: University Associates Press, 1969), pp. 52-57.

Process

I. Each participant is given a copy of the individual work sheet and told that he has fifteen minutes to complete the exercise.

II. One group work sheet is handed to each group.

    A. Individuals are not to change any answers on their individual sheets as a result of group discussion.

    B. A member of the group is to record group consensus on this sheet.

    C. The participants will have thirty minutes in which to complete the group work sheet.

III. Each participant is given a copy of the direction sheet for scoring. This phase of the experience should take seven to ten minutes.

    A. They are to score their individual work sheets.

    B. They will then give their score to the recorder, who will compute the average of the individual scores.

    C. The recorder will then score the group work sheet.

IV. The group will compute the average score for individuals with the group score and discuss the implications of the experience. This phase of the experience should take seven to ten minutes.

V. Results are posted according to the chart below, and the facilitator directs a discussion of the outcomes of consensus-seeking and the experience of negotiating agreement. Results are also compared to intragroup conflict intensities.

	Group 1	Group 2	Group 3
Consensus Score			
Average Score			
Range of Individual Scores			

NASA EXPERIMENT INDIVIDUAL WORKSHEET

Instructions: You are a member of a space crew originally scheduled to rendezvous with a mother ship on the lighted surface of the moon. Due to mechanical difficulties, however, your ship was forced to land at a spot some 200 miles from the rendezvous point. During landing, much of the equipment aboard was damaged, and, since survival depends on reaching the mother ship, the most critical items available must be chosen for the 200 mile trip. Below are listed the 15 items left intact and un-damaged after landing. Your task is to rank order them in terms of their importance to your crew in allowing them to reach the rendezvous point. Place the number 1 by the most important item, the number 2 by the second most important, and so on, through number 15, the least important. *You have 15 minutes to complete this phase of the exercise.*

_____ Box of matches
_____ Food concentrate
_____ 50 feet of nylon rope
_____ Parachute silk
_____ Portable heating unit
_____ Two .45 calibre pistols
_____ One case dehydrated Pet milk
_____ Two 100-lb. tanks of oxygen
_____ Stellar map (of the moon's constellation)
_____ Life raft
_____ Magnetic compass
_____ 5 gallons of water
_____ Signal flares
_____ First aid kit containing injection needles
_____ Solar-powered FM receiver-transmitter

NASA EXPERIMENT GROUP WORKSHEET

Instructions: This is an exercise in group decision-making. Your group is to employ the method of *Group Consensus* in reaching its decision. This means that the prediction for each of the fifteen survival items must be agreed upon by each group member before it becomes a part of the group decision. Consensus is difficult to reach. Therefore, not every ranking will meet with everyone's complete approval. Try, as a group, to make each ranking one with which all group members can at least partially agree. Here are some guides to use in reaching consensus:

1. Avoid arguing for your own individual judgments. Approach the task on the basis of logic.
2. Avoid changing your mind only in order to reach agreement and avoid conflict. Support only solutions with which you are able to agree somewhat, at least.
3. Avoid "conflict-resolution" techniques such as majority vote, averaging, or trading in reaching your decision.
4. View differences of opinion as helpful rather than as a hindrance in decision-making.

_____ Box of matches
_____ Food concentrate
_____ 50 feet of nylon rope
_____ Parachute silk
_____ Portable heating unit
_____ Two .45 calibre pistols
_____ One case dehydrated Pet milk
_____ Two 100-lb. tanks of oxygen
_____ Stellar map (of moon's constellation)
_____ Life raft
_____ Magnetic compass
_____ 5 gallons of water
_____ Signal flares
_____ First aid kit containing injection needles
_____ Solar-powered FM receiver-transmitter

EXERCISE 3: GROUP RANKING TASK *

Goals

   I. To compare the results of individual decision-making with decisions made by groups.

  II. To generate data to discuss decision-making patterns in task groups.

Group Size

Between six and twelve participants. Several groups may be directed simultaneously in the same room.

Time Required

Approximately one hour.

Process

   I. Each participant is given a copy of the Occupational Prestige Ranking Worksheet and is told that he has seven minutes to complete the task. He must work independently during this phase.

* *Source:* J. William Pfeiffer and John E. Jones, *A Handbook of Structured Experiences for Human Relations Training, Vol. II* (Iowa City: University Associates Press, 1970), pp. 22-24.

II.   After seven minutes, the facilitator asks that a ranking be made by the total group, using the method of group consensus. The ranking of each occupation must be agreed upon by each member before it becomes a part of the group's decision. Members should try to make each ranking one with which all members agree at least partially. Two ground rules: no averaging, and no "majority rule" votes. The group has thirty minutes to complete its task.

III. After thirty minutes of group work (or when the group has finished, if less than thirty minutes), the facilitator should announce the "correct" ranking.** Individual group members should "score" their worksheets by adding up the differences between their ranks and the key, regardless of sign. That is, make all differences positive and sum them. Low scores, of course, are better than high ones. Someone should score the group ranking also.

IV.   The group should compute the average score of the individual members, compare this with the group's score, and discuss the implications of the experience. Results are also compared to intragroup conflict intensities.

OCCUPATIONAL PRESTIGE RANKING WORKSHEET

Instructions: Rank the following occupations according to the prestige that is attached to them in the United States. Place a "1" in front of the occupation that you feel to be most prestigious, etc., all the way to "15," least prestigious.

_____ Author of novels
_____ Newspaper columnist
_____ Policeman
_____ Banker
_____ U.S. Supreme Court Justice
_____ Lawyer
_____ Undertaker
_____ State governor
_____ Sociologist
_____ Scientist
_____ Public school teacher
_____ Dentist
_____ Psychologist
_____ College Professor
_____ Physician

** Prestige scores based on Occupational Prestige in the United States: 1925-1963 in R. Bendix and S. M. Lipset, eds., *Class, Status, and Power,* 2nd ed. (New York: The Free Press, 1966), pp. 322-34.

EXERCISE 4: FUNCTIONAL OR DYSFUNCTIONAL?

Goal

To compare functional and dysfunctional forms of conflict.

Group Size

From three to five. Several groups may be directed simultaneously.

Time Required

Approximately forty-five minutes.

Process

I.   Each participant analyzes the four conflict situations on an individual basis and circles that response to each situation that he believes represents the most effective solution.

II. The group as a whole then analyzes the various responses made to each question. In which situations is the conflict functional? Dysfunctional?

III. What choice or choices should the effective conflict manager have chosen/avoided?

SITUATIONS

1. A group of your friends is watching a television program in your home. Two of the people are having an argument which becomes so loud

that the rest of the group cannot hear the television. How would you react to this situation?

    a.   Tell the two people to leave the room; or tell them to be quiet.

    b.   Tell the two people to lower their voices; or ask them to quit arguing; or ask them to leave the room.

    c.   Ask them to lower their voices.

    d.   Ask the group to move closer to the TV; or turn up the volume.

    e.   Do nothing; turn off the TV; or leave the room yourself.

    f.   _____.

2.   You are the moderator in a group session with five other people. The purpose of the session is to formulate a plan that requires consent from all participants. One of the participants is so involved with the important details of the plan that he is delaying the group from reaching agreement. As moderator, what would you do in this situation?

    a.   Tell him to be quiet; or tell him to leave the group.

    b.   Ignore him; or persuade him to ignore the details.

    c.   Postpone the discussion of the details until a later time.

    d.   Allow limited discussion.

    e.   Try to understand what the participant has to say; or let the person have the floor and explain his position.

    f.   _____.

3.   Your boss has called you into his office and you find that he wants your opinion about the performance of one of your co-workers. The co-worker is your best friend and neighbor, but you are inclined to believe that his performance is substandard. What would you tell the boss?

    a.   Request that the boss ask the co-worker to join the discussion.

    b.   Explain to the boss that you understand the situation, but he is your best friend and you could not be unbiased in your opinion.

    c.   Give no opinion.

    d.   In discussion point out the co-worker's good and poor work habits.

    e.   Talk around the issue.

    f.   _____.

4.   You are a staff specialist and have been assigned two projects: one by your immediate supervisor and one by the supervisor of another department. There is adequate time to complete both projects by the

deadline date, however, neither project would be completed with the degree of excellence required by your organization. What would you do?

a. Ask one or another of the supervisors for assistance.
b. Tell only one of the supervisors about the problem.
c. Contact both supervisors involved and tell them about your problem.
d. Do either one or another of the projects first without contacting either of the supervisors.
e. Do nothing about the problem; or complete both projects within the deadline date.
f. _____.

EXERCISE NO. 5: CHANGE IN LEADERSHIP

Goal

To develop and analyze a conflict environment brought about by a change in leadership style.

Time Required

Approximately one hour.

Group Size

Nine participants: the owner-manager, two cooks, four waitresses/ waiters, and two bus girls/boys.

Situation

The "owner-manager" has just purchased a restaurant and plans to manage it himself. The restaurant opened five years ago with the same eight employees that are currently working there. The employees were all quite young when the restaurant first opened; none of the staff is over 30 years of age today.

The restaurant earned a reasonable profit for the previous owner. But, this prior owner-manager was an authoritarian. The new owner believes he can improve the restaurant's overall performance by changing the leadership environment through use of a participative style. He decides to call the entire staff together on his first day in the restaurant and present to them his new way of operating.

Process

I. Assign each member of the group one of the nine roles: owner-manager, cook (2), waitress/waiter (4), and bus girl/boy (2).

II. On fourteen slips of paper, write each of the following role descriptions twice:
   A. Logician: Purely rational. Logical arguments are the only influence upon you.
   B. Status Quo Advocator: Doesn't want any kind of change.
   C. Crisis Lover: Achieves great satisfaction when things are in chaos.
   D. Antagonist: Purposely provokes all kinds of conflict.
   E. Smoother: All Differences can be smoothed over. Emphasizes similarities.
   F. Agreer: Diplomat. Can agree with everyone.
   G. Compromiser: All differences can be resolved through compromise.

III. Fold papers so description is concealed. Mix the slips thoroughly and have each of the eight "employees" select a role description.

IV. Each of the eight employees now has a title and a behavioral role to play. Additionally, each of the eight has some basic similarities: All are under 30. They have known only one type of leadership during the past five years—being told what to do. More specifically, they have seen the success of having "one man call all the shots."

   The owner-manager's role is that of a strong supporter of participative management.

V. Role play for half an hour.

VI. Discuss:
   A. Methods used by the owner to stimulate conflict and change.
   B. Forms of resistance and support shown by employees.
   C. Relevance of roles played by participants to "real life" behavior.

Selected Bibliography

Aldrich, Howard, "Organizational Boundaries and Inter-organizational Conflict," *Human Relations,* August, 1971, pp. 279-93.

Argyris, Chris, *Integrating the Individual and the Organization.* New York: John Wiley and Sons, 1964.

Assael, Henry, "Constructive Role of Inter-organizational Conflict," *Administrative Science Quarterly,* December, 1969, pp. 573-82.

Bailey, Stephen K., "Preparing Administrators for Conflict Resolution," *Educational Record,* Summer, 1971, pp. 233-39.

Barnard, Chester I., *The Functions of the Executive.* Cambridge: Harvard University Press, 1938.

Bennis, Warren G., Kenneth D. Benne, and Robert Chin, eds., *The Planning of Change* (2nd ed.), New York: Holt, Rhinehart & Winston, Inc., 1969.

Benton Lewis R., "The Many Faces of Conflict," *Supervisory Management,* March, 1970, pp. 7-10.

Berlo, David K., *The Process of Communication.* New York: Holt, Rinehart & Winston, Inc., 1960.

Bernard, Jessie, T. H. Pear, Raymond Aron, and Robert C. Angell, *The Nature of Conflict.* Paris: UNESCO, 1957.

Binzen, Peter and Joseph R. Daughen. *Wreck of the Penn Central*. Boston: Little, Brown and Company, 1971.

Blake, Robert R. and Jane S. Mouton, *Managerial Grid*. Houston: Gulf Publishing Co., 1964.

————, Herbert A. Shepard, and Jane S. Mouton, *Managing Intergroup Conflict in Industry*. Houston: Gulf Publishing Co., 1964.

Boulding, Kenneth J., *Conflict and Defense: A General Theory*. New York: Harper & Row Publishers, Inc., 1962.

————, "Organization and Conflict," *Journal of Conflict Resolution*. June, 1957, pp. 122-34.

Burke, Ronald J., "Methods of Resolving Superior-Subordinate Conflict: The Constructive Use of Subordinate Differences and Disagreements," *Organizational Behavior and Human Performance*. July, 1970, pp. 393-411.

————, "Methods of Resolving Interpersonal Conflict," *Personnel Administration*. July, 1969, pp. 48-55.

Coleman, James S., *Community Conflict*. New York: Free Press of Glencoe, 1957.

Corwin, Ronald G., "Patterns of Organizational Conflict," *Administrative Science Quarterly*. December, 1969, pp. 507-20.

Coser, Lewis, *The Functions of Social Conflict*. New York: Free Press of Glencoe, 1956.

Dahrendorf, Ralf, *Class and Class Conflict in Industrial Society*. London: Routledge and Kegan Paul, 1959.

Dalton, Gene W., Louis B. Barnes, and Abraham Zaleznick, *The Distribution of Authority in Formal Organization*. Boston: Division of Research, Graduate School of Business Administration, Harvard University, 1968.

Dalton, Melville, *Men Who Manage*. New York: John Wiley & Sons, Inc., 1959.

Dearborn, DeWitt C. and Herbert A. Simon, "Selected Perception: A Note on the Department Identifications of Executives," *Sociometry*. June, 1958, pp. 140-44.

DeKadt, E. J., "Conflict and Power in Society," *International Social Science Journal*. XVII, No. 3, 1965, pp. 454-71.

Deutsch, Morton, "Conflicts: Productive and Destructive," *Journal of Social Issues*. January, 1969, pp. 7-41.

Dutton, John M. and Richard E. Walton, "Interdepartmental Conflict and Cooperation: Two Contrasting Studies," *Human Organization*. Fall, 1966, pp. 207-21.

Ephron, Lawrence R., "Group Conflict in Organizations: A Critical Appraisal of Recent Theories," *Berkeley Journal of Sociology*. Spring, 1961, pp. 53-72.

Evan, William M., "Conflict and Performance in R & D Organizations," *Industrial Management Review.* Fall, 1965, pp. 37-46.

Fink, Clinton F., "Some Conceptual Difficulties in the Theory of Social Conflict," *Journal of Conflict Resolution.* December 1968, pp. 412-60.

Fox, Alan, "Coming to Terms With Conflict," *Personnel Management.* June, 1972, pp. 20-23.

Frederickson, H. George, "Role Occupancy and Attitudes Toward Labor Relations in Government," *Administrative Science Quarterly.* December, 1969, pp. 595-606.

Gross, Bertram M., *The Managing of Organizations.* New York: Free Press of Glencoe, 1964.

Hacon, Richard J., *Conflict and Human Relations Training.* Oxford: Pergamon Press, 1965.

Hall, Jay and Martha S. Williams, "A Comparison of Decision-Making Performances in Established and Ad Hoc Groups," *Journal of Personality and Social Psychology.* February, 1966, pp. 214-22.

Hayakawa, S. I., *Language in Thought and Action.* New York: Harcourt Brace Jovanovich Inc., 1949.

Johnson, David W., "Students Against the School Establishment: Crisis Intervention in School Conflict and Organization Change," *Journal of School Psychology.* IX, No. 1, 1971, pp. 84-91.

Janis, Irving L., "Groupthink," *Psychology Today.* November, 1971, pp. 43-46, 74-76.

Kahn, Robert L. and Elise Boulding, *Power and Conflict in Organizations.* New York: Basic Books, Inc., 1964.

————, D. M. Wolfe, R. P. Quinn, J. D. Snoek, and R. A. Rosenthal, *Organizational Stress: Studies in Role Conflict and Ambiguity.* New York: John Wiley & Sons, Inc., 1964.

Katz, Daniel and Robert L. Kahn, *The Social Psychology of Organizations.* New York: John Wiley & Sons, Inc., 1966.

Kelly, Joe, *Organizational Behaviour.* Homewood, Illinois: Richard D. Irwin, Inc., 1969.

Landsberger, Henry A., "The Horizontal Dimension in Bureaucracy," *Administrative Science Quarterly.* December, 1961, pp. 299-332.

Lammers, Cornelis J., "Strikes and Mutinies: A Comparative Study of Organizational Conflicts Between Rulers and Ruled," *Administrative Science Quarterly.* December, 1969, pp. 558-72.

Lawrence, Paul R. and Jay W. Lorsch, *Organization and Environment.* Boston: Division of Research, Graduate School of Business Administration, Harvard University, 1967.

Leavitt, Harold J. and Lewis R. Pondy, *Readings in Managerial Psychology*. Chicago: University of Chicago Press, 1964.

Likert, Rensis, *New Patterns of Management*. New York: McGraw-Hill Book Company, 1961.

Litterer, Joseph A., "Conflict in Organization: A Re-examination," *Academy of Management Journal*. September, 1966, pp. 178-86.

Litwak, Eugene, "Models of Bureaucracy Which Permit Conflict," *American Journal of Sociology*. September, 1961, pp. 177-84.

Lorsch, Jay W. and Paul R. Lawrence, eds., *Managing Group and Intergroup Relations*. Homewood, Illinois: Richard D. Irwin, Inc., 1972.

Lowell, Jon, "GMAD: Lowdown at Lordstown," *Ward's Auto World*. April, 1972, pp. 27-31.

McClelland, C. A., "The Reorientation of the Sociology of Conflict: A Review," *Journal of Conflict Resolution,* March, 1962, pp. 88-95.

McNeil, Elton B., ed., *The Nature of Human Conflict*. Englewood Cliffs, New Jersey: Prentice-Hall, Inc., 1965.

Mack, Raymond W. and Richard C. Snyder, "The Analysis of Social Conflict—Toward an Overview and Synthesis," *Journal of Conflict Resolution*. June, 1957, pp. 212-48.

March, James G. and Herbert A. Simon, *Organizations*. New York: John Wiley & Sons, Inc., 1958.

Maslow, Abraham, *Eupsychian Management*. Homewood, Illinois: Richard D. Irwin, Inc., 1965.

Megginson, Leon C. and C. Ray Gullett, "A Predictive Model of Union-Management Conflict," *Personnel Journal*. June, 1970, pp. 495-503.

Miller, E. J., "Technology, Territory, and Time," *Human Relations*. August 1959, pp. 243-72.

Nierenberg, Gerard I., *The Art of Negotiating*. New York: Hawthorn Books, Inc., 1968.

Pondy, Louis R., "Organizational Conflict: Concepts and Models," *Administrative Science Quarterly*. September, 1967, pp. 296-320.

————, "Varieties of Organizational Conflict," *Administrative Science Quarterly*. December, 1969, pp. 499-505.

Rapoport, Anatol, *Fights, Games, and Debates*. Ann Arbor: University of Michigan Press, 1960.

Rausch, Erwin and Wallace Wohlking, *Handling Conflict in Management: A Business Game*. Westbury, New York: Didactic Game Co., 1969.

Rhenman, Eric, Lennart Stromberg, and Gunnar Westerlund, *Conflict and Cooperation in Business Organizations*. London: Wiley-Interscience, 1970.

Rico, Leonard, "Organizational Conflict: A Framework for Reappraisal," *Industrial Management Review*. Fall, 1964, pp. 67-80.

————, "The Clash of Hierarchies," *Industrial Management Review*. Spring, 1965, pp. 105-12.

Saville, Anthony, "Conflict: New Emphasis in Leadership," *The Clearing House*. September, 1971, pp. 52-55.

Schelling, Thomas C., *The Strategy of Conflict*. Cambridge: Harvard University Press, 1960.

Scott, William G., *The Management of Conflict*. Homewood, Illinois: Richard D. Irwin, Inc., 1965.

Seiler, J. A., "Diagnosing Interdepartmental Conflict," *Harvard Business Review*. September/October, 1963, pp. 121-32.

Selznick, Phillip, *TVA and the Grass Roots*. Berkeley: University of California, 1953.

Sherif, Muzafer, *In Common Predicament: Social Psychology of Intergroup Conflict and Cooperation*. Boston: Houghton Mifflin Co., 1966.

————, *Intergroup Relations and Leadership*. New York: John Wiley & Sons, Inc., 1962.

———— and Carolyn W., *Groups in Harmony and Tension*. New York: Harper and Brothers, 1953.

Simmel, Georg, *Conflict*. New York: Free Press of Glencoe, 1955.

Simon, Herbert A., *Administrative Behavior*. New York: The Macmillan Co., 1947.

Singer, K., *The Idea of Conflict*. Melbourne: Melbourne University Press, 1949.

Smith, Clagett G., "A Comparative Analysis of Some Conditions and Consequences of Intra-Organizational Conflict," *Administrative Science Quarterly*. March, 1966, pp. 504-529.

————, ed., *Conflict Resolution: Contributions of the Behavioral Sciences*. Notre Dame: University of Notre Dame Press, 1971.

Stagner, Ross, ed., *The Dimensions of Human Conflict*. Detroit: Wayne State University Press, 1967.

Strauss, George, "Tactics of Lateral Relationship: The Purchasing Agent," *Administrative Science Quarterly*. September, 1962, pp. 161-86.

————, "Work-flow Frictions, Interfunctional Rivalry, and Professionalism: A Case Study of Purchasing Agents," *Human Organization*. Summer, 1964, pp. 137-49.

———— and Eliezer Rosenstein, "Workers Participation: A Critical View," *Industrial Relations*. February, 1970, pp. 197-214.

Summers, David A., "Conflict, Compromise, and Belief Change in a Decision-Making Task," *Journal of Conflict Resolution.* June, 1968, pp. 215-21.

Tannenbaum, Robert and Warren H. Schmidt, "Management of Differences," *Harvard Business Review.* November/December, 1960, pp. 107-15.

───── and Warren H. Schmidt, "How to Choose a Leadership Pattern," *Harvard Business Review.* March/April, 1958, pp. 95-101.

Thelen, Herbert A., *Dynamics of Groups at Work.* Chicago: University of Chicago Press, 1954.

Thompson, James D., *Organizations in Action.* New York: McGraw-Hill Book Company, 1967.

Thompson, Victor A., *Modern Organization.* New York: Alfred A. Knopf, Inc., 1964.

Urwick, Lyndall, *The Elements of Administration.* New York: Harper and Brothers, 1943.

Walton, Richard E., *Interpersonal Peacemaking: Confrontations and Third-Party Consultation.* Reading, Massachusetts: Addison-Wesley Publishing Co., 1969.

───── and John M. Dutton, "The Management of Interdepartmental Conflict: A Model and Review," *Administrative Science Quarterly.* March, 1969, pp. 73-84.

───── John M. Dutton and Thomas P. Cafferty, "Organizational Context and Interdepartmental Conflict," *Administrative Science Quarterly.* December, 1969, pp. 522-42.

Walton, Richard E. and R. B. McKensie, eds., *A Behavioral Theory of Labor Negotiations.* New York: McGraw-Hill Book Company, 1965.

Warren, Donald I., "The Effects of Power Bases and Peer Group on Conformity in Formal Organizations," *Administrative Science Quarterly.* December, 1969, pp. 544-56.

Weber, Max, *From Max Weber: Essays in Sociology,* trans., by H. H. Gerth and C. Wright Mills. New York: Oxford University Press, 1946.

White, Harrison, "Management Conflict and Sociometric Structure," *American Journal of Sociology.* September, 1961, pp. 185-99.

Whyte, William F., *Human Relations in the Restaurant Industry.* New York: McGraw-Hill Book Company, 1948.

Wright, Quincy, "The Nature of Conflict," *The Western Political Quarterly.* June, 1951, pp. 193-209.

Zald, Mayer N., "Power Balance and Staff Conflict in Correctional Institutions," *Administrative Science Quarterly.* June, 1962, pp. 22-49.

Ziller, Robert C., Harmon Zeigler, Gary L. Gregor, Richard A. Styskal, and Wayne Peak, "The Neutral in a Communication Network Under Conditions of Conflict," *American Behavioral Scientist.* November/December, 1969, pp. 265-82.

Index

DATE DUE

OCT 19 82 MAR 0 4 1992		
NOV 16 MAY 2 5 1992		
NOV 28 82 NOV 3 0 1992		
DEC 10 82 MAY 1 6 1994		
DEC 7 1994 OCT 0 8 1994	OCT 2 3 1994	
AUG 1 5 88 JUL 2 2 1988		
FEB 24 1989 NOV		
OCT 2 8 1991 NOV 1 3 1994		
NOV 0 5 1991		
DEC 0 9 1991 NOV 1 7 1995		